PHILLIES
CONFIDENTIAL

THE UNTOLD INSIDE STORY OF THE
2008 CHAMPIONSHIP SEASON

Gary Matthews
with Scott Lauber

TRIUMPH
BOOKS

This book is available in quantity at special discounts for your
group or organization. For further information, contact:

Triumph Books
542 South Dearborn Street
Suite 750
Chicago, Illinois 60605
(312) 939-3330
Fax (312) 663-3557

Printed in U.S.A.
ISBN: 978-1-60078-202-2
Editorial and page production by Prologue Publishing
Services, LLC.
Photos courtesy of AP Images unless otherwise indicated.

To my family, friends, and Phillies fans everywhere.
— G.M.

For Dad, who began my baseball education
by taking me to my first game at Yankee Stadium;
and for Mom, who taught me everything else.
— S.L.

CONTENTS

PROLOGUE

For a moment—a few seconds, really—it is 1983 again.

Gary Matthews swaggers onto the field, his chest puffed out. He appears confident, even though his stomach is turning somersaults. Matthews, known throughout baseball as "Sarge," stops a few feet shy of the Phillies' dugout and stretches his right arm. He looks to the heavens, adjusts his hat, and surveys the boisterous sellout crowd, soaking in the familiar, three-syllable chant.

"Beat L.A! Beat L.A.!"

In '83, Sarge made sure the Phillies beat L.A. Facing the Dodgers in the National League Championship Series, he batted .429 (6-for-14) with three home runs and eight RBIs. His three-run blast gave the Phillies the lead in the first inning of series-clinching Game 4 at Veterans Stadium, and when it was over, he copped the NLCS MVP award—and the red 1983 Chevrolet Camaro that came with it.

Now, 25 years later, Sarge has moved from left field to the broadcast booth. He's a color commentator for the Phillies, who are back in the NLCS, facing the Dodgers again, before another raucous sellout crowd that is repeating that same rhythmic melody.

"Beat L.A.! Beat L.A!"

And there's Sarge, stylish as always, clad in a gray jacket, black shirt, black slacks, and his favorite fedora, striding to the mound at Citizens Bank Park with former Gold Glove center fielder Garry Maddox to throw the ceremonial first pitches.

Maddox goes first, short-arming a strike to catcher Chris Coste. Then, not waiting for public-address announcer Dan Baker to finish enunciating his high-pitched introduction, Sarge winds up, tosses a strike of his own, and waves to the roaring crowd.

"Beat L.A.! Beat L.A.!"

.   .   .   .

That was a little panic job going on. We were standing out there for a while, you know. Garry threw his first, then I threw before they said anything. Harry [Kalas, the Phillies' Hall of Fame play-by-play announcer] told me, "You've got to let them go through all of the different accolades and everything." So I think I kind of jumped the gun there. But it's an honor to be able to throw out the ball, and it just shows you that the organization respects you and remembers what you did for them. The crowd was really excited, with the rally towels going. You could hear the chant, "Beat L.A.! Beat L.A.!" It takes you back, definitely. It's hard to say if it was as loud or not because this stadium is more open than the Vet, but when you're part of the opposition, it's a chant you just don't want to hear. It reminds me of those Clydesdales in St. Louis, the

Tomahawk Chop in Atlanta. It just makes you feel ill when you hear those songs. So the heart was definitely going a little bit. It showed me I was more nervous than I even thought. I just had in the back of my mind that I wanted to get it there, don't make a spectacle of myself, tripping and falling or doing something crazy. I just went out there and winged it. I think Maddox may have been throwing some balls and warming up. Coming out, I was like, "Man, you're sweating away." Well, he was back there practicing. Anyway, it was a fun time.

•   •   •   •

To understand how these Phillies—and Sarge—got here, flash back 13 months.

On September 12, 2007, after a 12–0 pounding by the Colorado Rockies, the Phils trailed the New York Mets by seven games in the National League East standings. Jimmy Rollins's notorious off-season boast that the Phillies would be the "team to beat" in the division wasn't looking good, and the following night, as they packed for a 10-game road swing that would open at Shea Stadium, several players even conceded the division and turned their focus to the wild-card race.

"Not that you mean to do it, but, realistically, we have to shift our attention away from the Mets," left fielder Pat Burrell said. "If it happens, it happens. But seven games, at this point, that's tough, so we have to regroup and think about the wild card."

Coste added, "It's the facts. We unfortunately put ourselves in this hole to where the wild card seems like the way we have to do it."

But the Phillies swept three games from the Mets in New York, then won two of three in St. Louis and three of four in Washington. By the time they came home for the season's final week, the deficit was a more manageable 2½ games. And by September 27, after home runs by Ryan Howard and Burrell beat the Atlanta Braves and the free-falling Mets fell again, they were tied for first.

On the season's final day, the Mets surrendered seven first-inning runs against the Florida Marlins. Meanwhile, 44-year-old left-hander Jamie Moyer pitched the Phillies to a 6–1 victory over the Washington Nationals.

The improbable comeback—and, in New York, the epic collapse—was complete.

So the Phillies surprised even themselves. They went 13–4 in the last 17 games (the Mets went 5–12) and won the NL East for the first time since 1993. And although they got swept by the sizzling, wild-card-winning Rockies in the best-of-five NL Division Series, the euphoria of the season's final three weeks propelled them into an off-season of great promise.

$$\cdot \quad \cdot \quad \cdot \quad \cdot$$

To come back with 17 games to go, the Mets are up by seven games, that's the worst collapse of all time. Literally. They moved everybody over. I mean everybody—the '69 Cubs, the '64 Phillies, the '78 Red Sox, everybody. Look it up. I mean, it was awful. Late in the season, in talking a lot with Keith [Hernandez, the former Mets first baseman and current television commentator], he kept saying that he didn't like the look of that team, how they were playing. He could almost see it coming. We called and texted back and forth about it. Realizing that you're not playing, you don't take it the same way. But there's definitely some pride involved there because it's your former team. There were some tough losses there where the guys could've just folded up. But it just shows how good this team is at bouncing back. They only talk about wins. When you talk to them, it's not a "me" thing. It's about the team. It's like what Ryne Sandberg said in his Hall of Fame speech, and it's one of my favorite sayings. He said, "When did the name on the back [of the uniform] ever become more important than the name on the front?" There is none of that going on with this team. They respect each other too much, and they respect the game too much. But it was a great comeback, and it definitely meant a lot to the city and the franchise to get into the postseason.

Sometimes, you can be overjoyed when you win and forget there's more work to be done. I don't think that's what happened. I think they realized there was work to get done, but it just didn't happen or it just wasn't right. Like when we played Baltimore in '83 [in the World Series]. Winning the first game, but still having the lineup in disarray to where Maddox wasn't playing and so on, you tend to think about that, and you tend to think about that a lot.

Let's face it, they way they got pitched in the playoffs, and by those young guys like [Ubaldo] Jimenez, who weren't used to being quality major league pitchers, you almost have to say things were lined up for the Colorado Rockies to win it. They weren't going to lose. It definitely could be a good experience, going through it for the first time, as long as you get back. That's the hard part. It's a great feeling to get there, and sure, you want to go further. But now, you're 162 ballgames away. How about that? Now, you have to grind through 162 to get back there, and that's the tough part about it. That's what makes baseball so tough.

Chapter 1

The Off-Season

OCTOBER 9, 2007

PHILADELPHIA—Amid the elation of the division-clinching champagne party at Citizens Bank Park, team president David Montgomery lavished praise upon manager Charlie Manuel for directing the first-place finish despite a 4–11 start, a spate of injuries, and a patchwork pitching staff—all in the last year of his contract.

Tonight, Montgomery put the Phillies' money where his mouth was.

After joining his agent Pat Rooney in a long day of negotiations, Manuel signed a two-year, $3 million contract extension with a club option for 2010. The Phillies always wanted to retain Manuel, but with general manager Pat Gillick planning to step aside once his contract expires after the 2008 season, it wasn't certain they would make Manuel a multiyear offer. And after working all of 2007 as a lame duck, Manuel likely would've bristled at a one-year deal.

"I'm happy he's back," closer Brett Myers said. "I'm able to talk to Charlie about anything, and that's important. The fact is, he took us where we needed to be this year. Maybe not to the ultimate goal, but he got us into the playoffs. He kept this team together with all the injuries and kept the mood positive. It's good to know he'll do that for years to come."

Manuel, 63, wasn't the popular choice in November 2004. Fans wanted the Phillies to hire Jim Leyland, so they often derided Manuel for his Virginia twang and down-home personality and criticized his in-game strategy.

But he has steered the Phillies to a three-year record of 262–224, and last month, he reached the 250-win mark in fewer games than any manager in club history since Pat Moran in 1918. He's also the first Phillies manager to oversee three consecutive winning seasons since Danny Ozark (1975–1978).

And during the Phillies' on-field celebration of their unlikely division crown, fans finally saluted Manuel with chants of "Char-lie! Char-lie!"

Manuel's coaching staff—Rich Dubee (pitching), Milt Thompson (hitting), Jimy Williams (bench), Davey Lopes (first base), Steve Smith (third base), Ramon Henderson (bullpen), and Mick Billmeyer (catching)—also will return in 2008.

. . . .

I'm glad they brought him back. What he does is he brings a calmness to his baseball team. Not only that, he sticks to players. Like when Ryan Howard wasn't going good, people were saying, "Sit him down a day," or, "How can you keep playing him?" Then, he winds up with 40-something bombs and all that damage, and it's, like, okay. There are a few other managers you can put into that category. Bobby Cox, the respect that he gets from his players like [Tom] Glavine, [John] Smoltz, [Greg] Maddux, and the way that the players play.

Bobby understands that by letting guys do what they want, he'll get the most out of them, instead of someone coming in and saying, "Okay, no golf clubs on the plane." For me, it was always Bobby Cox, John McNamara. He was kind of a players' manager, too. He let you go out and play and let you do what you needed to do. It didn't matter back then with the Big Red Machine. They were just pouncing on guys. Those guys were an intimidating bunch. If you had mediocre pitchers, you got exploited. Plain and simple. They beat the heck out of you.

Regardless of whether they made the playoffs or not, I already saw the way players would play for Charlie. And besides that, the things that they say. At one particular point or another, he's probably had to get on each and every one of them—I'm talking about his superstars and so on, the guys who make the team really go. The intangible for the managers, a lot of times, is that they get stuck with players they don't particularly want. They have to prove to upper management that they're not really good players. A lot of times, upper management is making deals, and they're looking at paper and saying, "Here's a guy we want you to have," instead of asking guys who've been around a particular player or coach. How about gathering information? He's gotten stuck with some of those guys, and still, he's been able to overcome for whatever reason. Again, I'm sure Ryan obviously believes in his ability, but more importantly he is happy to be around someone who isn't fickle. All the guys appreciate that. That's the respect factor that he has. These guys have a tremendous amount of respect for each other, and that comes from Charlie. They never put the blame on anybody. They never say, "Can you believe this guy here can't do this?" How great is that? There's something to be said for that. Every team I've been on, you'll have guys who will say things about a player and the effort that he's giving or whatever. But I've never heard a guy say that here. When Charlie makes a move, they pat the other guy on the back and say, "Go get 'em." That comes down from Charlie. That's the effect he has.

NOVEMBER 7, 2007

ORLANDO—For months, the Phillies have been talking to the Houston Astros about trading for one of their relievers. Sometimes, they were focused on Dan Wheeler. Others, they discussed Chad Qualls. But there was one pitcher who really caught their attention.

Brad Lidge.

They finally got him.

Over lunch today at the general managers meetings in Orlando, assistant GM Ruben Amaro Jr. and new Astros GM Ed Wade worked out the framework for a deal that would send Lidge and utility infielder Eric Bruntlett to the Phillies for speedy outfielder Michael Bourn, reliever Geoff Geary, and third-base prospect Mike Costanzo. By evening, the trade was finalized.

In 2004 and 2005, Lidge was among baseball's most dominant closers, converting 71 saves in 79 chances and posting a 2.07 ERA. But he has struggled since surrendering Albert Pujols's titanic home run in Game 5 of the 2005 National League Championship Series. In the past two seasons, he has converted only 51 of 66 save chances and posted a 4.37 ERA.

The Phillies asked about Lidge in April, when their bullpen was such a mess that they turned Opening Day starter Brett Myers into a reliever. But then-Astros general manager Tim Purpura insisted on restoring Lidge's confidence, not trading

The Phillies acquired closer Brad Lidge from the Astros in an effort to strengthen their bullpen.

him. The Astros fired Purpura late in the season, and when Wade, the Phillies' former GM, got the job, he showed greater interest in dealing a reliever. The Phillies were content to start 2008 with Myers as their closer, but they concluded that the paper-thin free-agent market for starting pitching left them better suited to obtain a closer and move Myers back to the rotation.

Lidge, who made $5.35 million in 2007 and is due for a raise through salary arbitration, had knee surgery last month. Still feeling burned by the Chicago White Sox in the Freddy Garcia trade a year ago, the Phillies consulted Lidge's doctors and felt confident that he'll be ready for spring training. Phillies pro scout Gordon Lakey, a longtime advisor to GM Pat Gillick, also reported that Lidge's fastball velocity was up in September, an indication that his arm is healthy.

There was only one thing left to do.

Gillick and Charlie Manuel called Myers at his Jacksonville, Florida, home to make sure he was cool with moving back to the rotation. Myers, a starter throughout his career, has grown to relish the closer role and took great pride in recording the last out of the NL East–clinching victory. At first, Myers was shocked—"It was kind of like the phone went dead," Manuel said—but ultimately, he understood.

"We were able to fill two needs," Amaro said, "and we did it with one move."

· · · ·

Everybody knows the guy has a good arm. When I was coaching with the Cubs, he was lights-out whenever he came in against us. If you saw this guy in the ninth inning, I mean, it was game over. He's got a hard fastball and a really good slider. That's his bread-and-butter pitch. You hear guys talk about a change of scenery. I believe in that, absolutely. It does wonders for a lot of people. It could turn out to be a great thing for Michael Bourn. He wasn't going to play every day here. Now, he goes over to Houston, and he's their starting center fielder. So it's a real blessing for him. A lot of times, younger players don't always recognize that you don't get these opportunities to have a job given to you. Now, when it is, you have to work hard to keep it. Michael is lucky because they've got guys around him that can hit. All they're really asking him to do is catch the ball and run the bases, and we know he can do those things. We've seen him do it here. But, pretty soon, they're going to say, "Michael, we need you go chip in a few hits here." If he can get on, he can lead this league in stolen bases.

With Lidge, there's nothing wrong with his arm. We know that. He just needed to get the confidence back to the point where, during the last two years, maybe he wasn't throwing his fastball enough. He had something bad happen to him on the field, and maybe that shook his confidence a little bit. I mean, it's a humbling game. In Houston, for a while, the game was easy for him. You ask him the difference the last two years, he would probably say there's no difference except for him not making the pitches that he should've been making, maybe because he was hurting a little bit with the knee. But coming over here could be the best thing for him, and moving Brett back [to the rotation], you figure that should help, too.

NOVEMBER 10, 2007

PHILADELPHIA—If not for lefty reliever J.C. Romero pitching nearly every day during the final three weeks of last season, the Phillies almost certainly wouldn't have made the playoffs.

They rewarded him tonight with a new contract.

Less splashy than trading for Brad Lidge, but maybe equally important, the Phillies re-signed Romero to a three-year, $12 million deal with a $4.75 million club option for 2011. Had Romero hit the open market (the Phillies had two more days to negotiate exclusively with him), he likely would've had several suitors.

Not bad, considering he was unemployed five months ago.

Romero, 30, signed a minor league contract with the Phillies in late June after being released by the Boston Red Sox. In 51 games with the Phils, he posted a 1.24 ERA, limited left-handers to a .125 average (5-for-40), and stabilized a bullpen role that young lefties Matt Smith and Fabio Castro failed to fill earlier in the season.

·   ·   ·   ·

J.C. is a good pitcher, no doubt about it. But with some of the other situations that he was in, especially there in Boston, he was just not getting the opportunity. And, let's face it, being in the right place at the right time was big for him last year and pitching very well. Boston didn't have a spot for him, so the Phillies were able to cash in on that. That's how you find guys sometimes. To me, the good managers are good at that. They look at the stronger teams, the teams may have an abundance of talent in an area and have some decisions to make. You could see that J.C. pitches with a lot of heart, a lot of guts, and gets a lot of guys out on pitches that aren't strikes. The fact is, he can get that because he throws early strikes. We've seen him too when he's thrown strikes in a hitting count and come at them with fastballs, and they've been hit and hit hard. But he's smart enough to recognize that isn't the pitch he wants to throw. But, again, being the only lefty there, they really almost had no choice but to bring him back. They're going to have to have a lefty, if not two or maybe even three, in the bullpen. You need to have that. So they had to bring him back, especially with what he did down the stretch. He was an integral part of them making the playoffs.

NOVEMBER 20, 2007

PHILADELPHIA—After being crowned National League MVP last year, Ryan Howard noticed a change in the way people treated him. For one thing, he began getting recognized wherever he went.

Jimmy Rollins doubts that will happen to him.

"Fortunately," Rollins said, "I'm still under 5'7". So I can hide behind a lot of people."

But in 2007 the smallest of the Phillies made the biggest impact. Rollins started every game and played all but 17 innings. He was a Gold Glove shortstop and became the first player with at least 200 hits, 30 doubles, 15 triples, 30 home runs, and 30 stolen bases in a season.

Oh, he also boasted in January that the Phils would be the "team to beat" in the NL East.

Then he delivered.

For all that, Rollins was anointed today as the NL MVP by the Baseball Writers Association of America, receiving 16 of 32 first-place votes and edging Colorado Rockies slugger Matt Holliday by 17 points in the closest balloting since Terry Pendleton defeated Barry Bonds by 15 points in 1991.

"Jimmy Rollins labeled the Phillies the 'team to beat' in the NL East, and then he backed it up," said voter Adam Rubin of the *New York Daily News*. "He particularly rose to the occasion in head-to-head matchups with the Mets, batting .346. That's what an MVP does."

Rollins, 30, batted .335 with 31 runs, eight home runs, and 22 RBIs over the final 34 games, and in the season finale, he singled, stole two bases, scored in the first inning, and added an RBI triple to help the Phillies clinch the NL East title. Overall, he batted .296 with 38 doubles, 20 triples, 30 homers, 94 RBIs, and 41 steals.

"He just overall carried us," right fielder Shane Victorino said. "He said from day one that we were the team to beat, and he led us all the way."

.   .   .   .

I'm so happy that he won the MVP because he did just about everything that a guy can do in a season. Not only that, but he put the team on his shoulders when [Ryan] Howard was out, when [Chase] Utley was out. It started in spring training. He said, "We're the team to beat," and then he went out there and backed it up. In talking with him about it, I said, "The statement you made was great. And I don't think it's going to bother you, but it may bother some of your teammates because of the pressure." But he took away all of that with the way that he actually played and acted. In the first game in New York [in April], he made a big error, cost them the game, and then he stood up there and answered all those questions. I think the New York writers gained a lot of respect for Jimmy Rollins last year, and he got a lot of their votes because of what he said, because of the way he played, and because he was a stand-up guy when it came to answering all those questions. They never forgot that. He got a lot of votes with that. They were trying to give it to Holliday, and Holliday had a great year. But those guys knew what this kid here meant to the season and the league, from the triples and the doubles and the home runs to the excellent defensive play. He won a "triple crown"—Silver Slugger, Gold Glove, MVP. You can't do any better than that.

He brings something to the table. Fielding, obviously, he's a Gold Glover. Base running, he's a very smart base runner. It's his whole presence. I've likened him to Willie Mays because it's like everybody feels better when he's on the team. He does so many things to help your team win. I've told him that. He just smiles. When you're talking to a lot of guys one-on-one, you talk about how they could've played in that age. For me, J-Roll obviously has been told his whole life, "You can't do this. You're too small. You shouldn't play shortstop. Go to second base." But he's just a marvelous player. That's why the four [living] Philadelphia Negro Leagues guys [Harold Gould, Mahlon Duckett, Stanley Glenn, and Bill Cash] marvel over this guy because he reminds them of different people they played with. For J-Roll, who's not big in stature, what he does for his team, it just can't be measured. He definitely deserved the MVP because he had a great year. I don't think you could find a guy who was more valuable to his team.

DECEMBER 12, 2007

SAN FRANCISCO—During baseball's annual winter meetings last week in Nashville, general manager Pat Gillick said it was a "long shot" that the Phillies would re-sign Aaron Rowand. Deep down, though, he sensed the market for Rowand had begun receding. Fewer teams, it seemed, were willing to make a five-year offer to a free-agent center fielder whose hard-nosed style leaves him prone to injury.

The San Francisco Giants didn't care.

Rowand, 30, cashed in the finest season of his career today by signing a five-year, $60 million contract and will anchor a Giants lineup that scored the second-fewest runs in the National League last season and won't have Barry Bonds in 2008.

It is believed the Phillies were prepared to offer a three-year, $39 million contract. But Rowand wanted the security of a fifth year, even if it meant playing for a last-place team. And the Phillies wouldn't make a five-year commitment, even though Rowand played in 161 games last season.

So fleet-footed Shane Victorino will move from right field to center, his natural position, and the Phillies don't expect much of a defensive drop-off from Rowand, who won his first career Gold Glove. Jayson Werth will get more at-bats in right field and will be charged with helping to make up for Rowand's production from the right side of the plate.

But replacing their emotional leader won't be easy. Rowand endeared himself to fans by shattering his nose while running into the center-field wall to make a catch during a May 2006 game. He also was among the most vocal players in the clubhouse, a responsibility that seemingly will fall to back-to-back NL MVPs Ryan Howard and Jimmy Rollins and All-Star second baseman Chase Utley.

"Aaron is a great guy and an integral part of our success last year," assistant GM Ruben Amaro Jr. said. "But three years was the maximum we were prepared to go. We made an evaluation that we were putting ourselves at tremendous risk if we went more than three."

. . . .

I'm happy for Rowand. Now, at the same time, you know he's going to a team that probably won't be able to win consistently. But also knowing that, he's going to bring an aspect of toughness and, regardless, give it all he has. The money issue, we really can't know about that or get involved in that. Individually, I'm looking at this more as a coach or manager. Yes, I would really like to have him, understanding that I can't do anything that's going to jeopardize the club from doing what they need to do. They know full well how much Rowand meant to the club with how he played, but understandably, they weren't willing to go out on a limb for that amount of money with some other things happening—you've got Ryan Howard going to arbitration and so on.

But one of the intangibles on this ballclub, again, was Aaron Rowand. I don't think that anyone can overlook that. I think you realize how much he meant to this ballclub. Does that mean that the club should've paid him $60 million?

The Phillies lost their emotional leader when free-agent center fielder Aaron Rowand decided to sign with the San Francisco Giants.

Photo courtesy of Getty Images.

Absolutely not. But when you get rid of a guy, you hope you can get someone else who can give you the same. You might statwise, but heartwise, it doesn't measure up to what you have in center field. It's glaring. That's one thing about scouts and people who analyze things. They can't listen to a player's heart or determine how much desire he has. They could go on the ability or stats and say this is what he does. But stats don't tell the story. That's why Jamie Moyer is still able to play. He pitches with heart. It doesn't matter what hitter is up there. He doesn't back down. Yeah, Rowand probably would drop off during the fourth or fifth year, but the issue is whether he might get hurt. Do you want to say to a player, take it easy out there, don't get hurt? You can't have it both ways. You want players on your team who have character, who play hard. That was going to cost them a little bit too much. The way that management was thinking of it, Victorino could move to center field, you've got Jayson Werth in right. So they think they can make up for it.

DECEMBER 20, 2007

PHILADELPHIA—It didn't take long for the Phillies to find Aaron Rowand's replacement, although Geoff Jenkins doesn't see himself that way.

"I don't want to run into any walls or break a nose," said Jenkins, who finalized a two-year, $13 million contract with the Phillies today. "But I'm definitely an aggressive outfielder. I like diving and making catches at the wall and throwing guys out."

Jenkins, slated to split right field with righty-swinging Jayson Werth, will be asked to do all of those things. And in constructing their off-season plan, the Phillies targeted him from the start.

A streaky left-handed hitter with run-producing ability, Jenkins, 33, slipped into a three-way outfield platoon last season with the Milwaukee Brewers, who decided not to exercise his $9 million option. After belting 212 homers in 10 seasons with the Brewers (Sarge was his hitting coach in 2000), Jenkins was a free agent, and the Phillies saw similarities between him and Rowand.

But could they offer Jenkins enough at-bats? And could they outbid the San Diego Padres, whose sales pitch to the Phoenix-area resident included an Arizona spring-training site and perfect West Coast weather?

Then, earlier this week, the Padres dealt for Jim Edmonds, and Jenkins gravitated toward home run-friendly Citizens Bank Park. Charlie Manuel even made a recruiting call to help seal the deal.

"Once we lost Aaron, we definitely needed to pick up a guy that was established," Manuel said. "Jenkins is not only established, but I've liked the way he hits since he came up. He not only balances our lineup, he adds to it."

.   .   .   .

The intriguing thing for Geoff coming over is that, with the short porch in right field, there's a chance he might give you 20 home runs or so. But you wonder how well he'll fit in with this club because they have a lot of guys who strike out, and Geoff is a strikeout guy. To hit with consistency, you've got to have your body in the right position, and I think he would tell you he's had some problems with the stroke in the past. He might deny it himself, but he still has kind of an uppercut-type swing. When you do that, everything has to be perfect. Can you imagine an uppercut trying to hit a high fastball? It doesn't work. His best pitch is low, but sometimes, he swings it high. But, back then, Geoff was going to be playing every day, so you worked through it. What you'll have to do to him is move him to different spots in the lineup. You don't necessarily just take him out, as if he was some rookie who just got there and isn't getting paid a lot and doesn't have time in the league. All I know is that you can start wherever you want, like [Julio] Franco with your bat way up near your ear. All I'm looking at is when you're getting ready to get to the zone of that ball. If you're not there and you don't have that "V," the majority of the time in hitting, you're not going to be successful. Early on, he did that. But he was stronger, quicker. As you get older, you lose that. He'll have the opportunity to work on and to fix that. If it doesn't work, if he keeps the same batting stance and doesn't really change, then he won't have the success. And in order for you to see what kind of year this guy is going to have, he almost has to play every day because he's never really been a platoon guy before.

To say that he and Werth are going to replace Rowand, that doesn't tell the story. Because, again, Aaron was giving you clutch hits and giving you his whole heart and getting the job done. You would hope you get the same production, numbers-wise, but I don't even think you can compare the two because of the intangibles. That's like with the Cubs [in 2005]. They told me [Jason] Dubois and [Todd] Hollandsworth were going to do the same as Moises Alou. They said it would be better defense. I said, "I like the defense, but the other stuff ain't even close." You're talking about one of the better clutch hitters of all time. I was like, what are they smoking?

. . . .

Jenkins was the main attraction at today's press conference at Citizens Bank Park, but the Phillies also introduced Chad Durbin, a right-handed pitcher who signed for one year and $900,000. Durbin, 30, wasn't tendered a contract by the Detroit Tigers after finishing 8–7 with a 4.72 ERA in 36 games (19 starts) last season. He figures to push disappointing Adam Eaton for the number-five starter job during spring training, but he also may fit as a reliever.

. . . .

What I know about Durbin, he comes with a reputation of having a sharp slider and being able to throw two innings, and that can be huge when you're in the bullpen. I think it helps him maybe because he was a starter. A lot of times, when relievers get up, they get heated and then not brought in. That's damn near like throwing. Now add that up over the course of the year. That definitely takes its toll, so having a versatile guy who can throw a lot out there can be a big thing.

JANUARY 31, 2008

PHILADELPHIA—A few minutes after Pedro Feliz tried on his new red-pinstriped jersey today at Citizens Bank Park, assistant general manager Ruben Amaro Jr. said he believes the Phillies have "the best infield in Major League Baseball."

The New York Mets responded by trading for arguably the majors' best pitcher.

In the ongoing chess match between National League East rivals, the Mets pulled off the winter's biggest trade, shipping center-field prospect Carlos Gomez and three minor league pitchers to the Minnesota Twins for two-time Cy Young Award winner Johan Santana, then signing Santana to a six-year, $137.5 million contract extension.

The Phillies, meanwhile, signed free-agent third baseman Pedro Feliz to a two-year, $8.5 million deal and added him to an infield that features two NL MVPs (first baseman Ryan Howard and shortstop Jimmy Rollins) and the majors' best second baseman (Chase Utley). Feliz, known for his slick defense, has hit at least 20 homers in four consecutive seasons while playing his home games in San Francisco's cavernous AT&T Park. In their homer-friendly ballpark, the Phillies believe Feliz can belt 25 to 30 homers.

And Santana? If the Phillies are worried about him, they aren't admitting it.

"There's no question [Santana] is going to help their ballclub," Amaro Jr. said. "He's going to help them. He's one of the best pitchers in the game, there's no question about that. But we can't worry about what other clubs are doing around us. We have to concentrate on improving our club."

. . . .

Getting Santana, it's huge. No doubt, whenever you can bring in a pitcher of that magnitude, it makes you the favorite again. He's a great pitcher. You can't go out and get a better pitcher than that. When you're facing a [Don] Drysdale or [Sandy] Koufax or whatever, you're not feeling very good about that game. But the thing you have to remember is that it's only one game. He can't pitch every day.

Feliz is steady with the glove. You'd think he should hit about 25 or 30 home runs here in this ballpark, easy. From Dusty Baker, I've heard a lot about him. He said, "Wait until you see this guy field." The thing is his accuracy with his throws is very good. Dusty said he's a line-drive hitter, hits the ball to left-center. If he does it more, he'll hit more balls out. He said he's a good player to have on the team, doesn't complain. It's a little surprising the Giants didn't bring him back. But keep in mind now, this kid wanted a two- or three-year deal, one of those, and I don't know if the Giants were willing to do that, especially after they signed [Aaron] Rowand. They've invested in the pitcher, [Barry] Zito. So, I don't know if they had the money to bring back Feliz. If they had a kid in the minor leagues who could come in, that's probably the direction they're going to go in. They know they're not going to be able to win anyway. So why bring him back? But he should help out here. He should be good for this team.

Chapter 2

SPRING TRAINING

FEBRUARY 16, 2008

CLEARWATER, Florida—Pitchers and catchers have begun working out under the Florida sun. Position players are trickling into camp. Spring training has sprung, and the Phillies, defending division champions for the first time since 1993, couldn't be any more relaxed.

This morning, Kyle Kendrick even got Punk'd.

It began with a meeting in Charlie Manuel's office. Assistant general manager Ruben Amaro Jr. told Kendrick, a fresh-faced 23-year-old pitcher, that he'd been traded to the Yomiuri Giants of the Japanese Central League for Kobayashi Iwamura, a fictional pitcher. Amaro even handed Kendrick a letter that authorized the deal, and team travel director Frank Coppenbarger reviewed his itinerary.

Kendrick, last season's feel-good story after being unexpectedly called up at midseason and winning 10 games, left the office dazed and very confused. He called his agent, Joe Urban, who played along with the ruse. Then Amaro informed reporters, who also had been clued in to the prank and conducted a mock press conference with Kendrick.

"I don't know what to think right now," he stammered.

"You've been Punk'd," howled pitcher Brett Myers, ring-leader of the gag.

Hilarity ensued. Kendrick breathed a sigh of relief.

"I've never been so happy," he said.

The prank, filmed by Comcast Sports Net, already has been posted on YouTube, and Myers and Kendrick will even be guests on *The Today Show* later this week. Meanwhile, around the clubhouse, players are wearing red T-shirts that feature a picture of shirtless slugger Pat Burrell doing dumbbell curls and the slogan "Man or Machine."

So are the Phillies feeling pressure to repeat as division champs?

Not yet.

.   .   .   .

That was good. That was funny to see them play that prank on Kendrick. As long as it wasn't played on me, those jokes are great, except if you're the person getting laughed at. That took some clever stuff. I've had some jokes played on me. Not to that magnitude or anything. In Chicago, the clubhouse, we used to have those director's chairs, and [Ryne] Sandberg all the time would pull those damn sticks out, and every day I'd come in and sit there and go right down on the bottom. Every damn day. You look over, and he's kind of smirking or whatever. After a while, you get ticked, and it's like you've got to check your stuff. Or you'd be sitting there on the bench, and [Rick] Sutcliffe was there with all that alcohol, and they put a match there and give you a hot foot. Stuff like that. It's like, what the hell? That's the way it was. You should see how quiet Sandberg was. I'd say, "How did you come up with that? I didn't know you talked." You'd never suspect it was him.

Bob Uecker, too, and the clubbie in Milwaukee, Phil Rozewicz, I got them to play golf one day. I pull up, and Ueck is putting his golf clubs in the car, so I go in to Google the directions. Phil comes out, drives my car away, and I don't know he's across the street. So I go to where the cabs are. I come out and say, "Hey, man, where's my car?" The guy says, "I don't know. Some guy got in it." I'm cursing, and Phil is across the street with his camera, getting me with my hands up and so on. Then Ueck comes over and says, "Hey, Sarge, what's the problem?" I said, "I think somebody stole my car." He says, "Man, my clubs were in there." I said, "Forget your clubs. My damn car has been stolen." Then Phil comes across the street, waving with his camera. I said, "Get your clubs out of here. We're not going golfing anymore." Like I said, I've had enough jokes being pulled on me to know it's easier to laugh when it's on somebody else. But it does show the mindset right now. The guys are loose, they're relaxed. But they'll get serious when the time comes, too.

FEBRUARY 17, 2008
PORT ST. LUCIE, Florida—Upon reporting for spring training today, soft-spoken New York Mets center fielder Carlos Beltran uncharacteristically did his best

impression of Jimmy Rollins. Only he bragged that the Mets, not the Phillies, are the "team to beat" in the NL East.

That's the easy part.

Now, Beltran must deliver.

After blowing a seven-game lead with only 17 games remaining last season in a collapse for the ages, the Mets traded for two-time Cy Young Award winner Johan Santana, fueling Beltran's confidence that they can unseat the Phillies for the division title.

"Without Santana, we felt as a team we have a chance to win our division," Beltran said. "With him now, I have no doubt that we're going to win our division. I have no doubt in that. We've got what it takes. So this year, to Jimmy Rollins, we are the team to beat."

Rollins's retort: "Has anyone ever heard of plagiarism?"

"The words came out of his mouth," Rollins continued. "There's nothing for me to say. What I said last year still rings true. My mind isn't going to change. After 162 games, we'll be looking to win the next 11 [in the playoffs]. There isn't a team in this division or the National League that's better than us."

．　．　．　．

I think Beltran is sincere because of Santana. If their other guys don't get hurt, now that they have Santana, they feel pretty confident, as well they should. But it's one thing in being sincere and saying it than it is in saying it and then being able to go back it up. I mean, J-Roll willed them to win last year, especially with [Chase] Utley getting hurt and [Ryan] Howard getting hurt. His reputation was on the line for saying that. Jimmy is smart. He chooses his words right in the arenas that he's in. There's no use in commenting on what Beltran said. We won it last year. You're still chasing us. So, you can say whatever you want to say. Basically, that's what J-Roll is saying. He might've said it but in a quiet way like, "We're the team to beat." J-Roll never backed down. He never backed off what he said. That shows you something, too. So, Beltran can say whatever he wants to say, but now, he's got to back it up. He's got to do his part now.

FEBRUARY 21, 2008

ST. PETERSBURG, Florida—A few minutes before 9:00 AM yesterday, Ryan Howard stepped out of his 2007 Cadillac Escalade and walked into the posh Renaissance Vinoy Hotel and Resort.

"How do I look?" he said, adjusting his gray pinstriped suit.

"Like a million bucks," an onlooker responded.

Howard is about to be worth much more than that.

One day after a four-hour hearing, a three-member panel has awarded Howard a $10 million arbitration settlement that shocked the Phillies and may have altered baseball's salary structure. The $10 million ruling is the highest annual salary won by a first-time arbitration-eligible player and came before Howard has accrued even three full years of major league service.

If Howard had lost the case, he would've made $7 million, still a substantial raise from his $900,000 salary in 2007.

Either way, Howard would've been able to buy many more stylish suits.

Less certain, though, is whether the hearing, in which Phillies officials and Howard's agent debated the slugger's value, will spark a rift between player and team. Typically, arbitration hearings aren't pleasant for players, who have to listen as their employer lists their faults as reasons to pay them less.

"It really wasn't contentious," said Tal Smith, the Houston Astros president and arbitration expert enlisted by the Phillies to formulate and present their case. "It's only a continuation of the debate the parties had during their negotiations. I don't think there's anything denigrating or demeaning at all."

"I don't know about that," a smiling Howard said after emerging from the hearing.

Howard's camp, led by agent Casey Close, argued that Howard has more homers (105) and RBIs (285) than any player over the past two seasons and referenced slugger Miguel Cabrera, who won his hearing and a $7.4 million award last year in his first arbitration go-around.

The Phillies' argument seemingly focused on Howard's limited major league service time. Although he has National League Rookie of the Year and MVP trophies on his mantle, players with such little experience don't often earn eight-figure annual salaries.

Howard, 28, will be 32 by the time he can become a free agent after the 2011 season. To avoid future arbitration battles, the Phils could sign him to a long-term contract. But he'd have to be willing to trade a few dollars for the security of a multiyear deal, and at this point, it doesn't appear that Howard is willing to do that.

. . . .

With the figures that I saw, I thought it was going to be automatic that he'd win the case. It may be automatic next year, too, depending on what happens. You're talking about 50 home runs, almost 150 RBIs, every year. The numbers speak for themselves. With what he does for a club, with the home runs, it enables the club to win games a little easier than when they have to be stringing together two or three hits at a time. Honestly, I don't look at it as a big deal. I think it becomes a story with a lot of the sportswriters, and well it should be. But

I've always been in tune that, no matter what you sign for, you've got to still come and play. It's really simple. His attitude has been, pay me now or pay me later, but you're paying me later now. It's up to [the Phillies] how they want to structure it and get it done. But the one thing that you have to know is that if it got to the point where he was a free agent, how many teams do you think would be at his doorstep? I think it would be a pretty long line. That's the whole scary thing about what the Phillies are going through right now.

But that's management's decision on that. Obviously, if they ever wanted to trade him or whatnot, you've got to feel there would be all the teams lined up that would really want him because of the home runs. They don't really get a chance to see as much of the other things, like the defense. But you can say whatever you want. He's a force to be reckoned with. He's still done just about better than anybody who's ever put on the uniform in the first three years and the fastest to 100 home runs and so forth. So that's saying something, and he's already won the MVP. Put him on the block and see how many people are going to step up, especially some of the American League clubs. The fact is, again, you've got to reckon with him, and with one swing, he's as dangerous as anybody, maybe more dangerous.

FEBRUARY 24, 2008

CLEARWATER, Florida—As he unleashed a pitch during a workout yesterday at the Carpenter Complex, Brad Lidge caught his spike on the mound and felt pain in his surgically repaired right knee. When he awoke today, it was sore and swollen.

And, tomorrow, he will have surgery.

Lidge, the Phillies' new closer, will undergo an arthroscopic procedure in Philadelphia to fix two tears in his meniscus, the moon-shaped cartilage in the knee. Team physician Dr. Michael Ciccotti will remove part of the meniscus, leaving Lidge sidelined for three to six weeks. In the interim, veteran Tom Gordon will serve as the closer.

On October 1, five weeks before being acquired by the Phils in a five-player deal with Houston, Lidge had surgery on torn cartilage in his knee. At the time, the Astros' medical staff decided to repair, not remove, the meniscus. By removing the damaged cartilage, Phillies doctors have assured Lidge that he won't have further pain or setbacks this season.

"We're still viewing this as a relatively short-term thing," assistant general manager Mike Arbuckle said. "Whenever we've dealt with this type of injury in the past, we've always had good return times. We don't think this is going to put him too far behind."

.   .   .   .

No, I'm not really too worried about it at all. It's not like they're saying he won't be back, and actually, he may be back even a little bit earlier than they're expecting initially here. Brad is a hard worker. He'll do what he needs to do to get back on the mound. And, again, it's not like he's coming here with a bad arm or anything. It's his knee. For them to go in and clean that up, that's going to be good for him.

FEBRUARY 26, 2008

CLEARWATER, Florida—When the Phillies won their first National League East title since 1993, Brett Myers threw the clinching pitch.

In five weeks, when they begin their title defense, Myers will throw the first pitch.

Before rain washed out the exhibition opener tonight against Florida State University, the Phillies named Myers as their starter for Opening Day, March 31, against the Washington Nationals at Citizens Bank Park, choosing him over ace left-hander Cole Hamels.

Nobody was more surprised than Myers.

"Absolutely," he said. "Hamels had a great year last year. I'm going to have to work that much harder to earn that spot."

Charlie Manuel and pitching coach Rich Dubee picked Myers, in part, to erase any doubts that he will remain in the rotation, even though new closer Brad Lidge will miss three to six weeks after having arthroscopic surgery this week on his right knee. Also, by making Myers their Opening Day starter, the Phillies are rewarding him for his willingness to return to the rotation after finishing last season as the closer, a role he grew to adore.

It will mark Myers's second straight Opening Day start. Last season, he made three starts before agreeing to become a reliever in mid-April to help fortify a beleaguered bullpen and taking over as closer in May when Tom Gordon went on the disabled list.

Myers called himself "a good 1-A guy," seemingly deferring the ace status to Hamels.

· · · ·

Hamels really didn't care. I think they just want to put Brett in a situation that really allows him to feel like he's the number-one guy. They want him to harness that. And they would rather him have that than even Cole. To me, Cole is confident no matter what. If you're number one or number two, you're still number one and number two because, any day, number two can be number one. It didn't bother Cole, I don't think. It's like I told my son after the Angels signed Torii Hunter. Whatever they ask you to do, do. You're under contract. If they ask you to pinch-run, go pinch-run. If they ask you to pinch-hit, go pinch-hit. I think for a pitcher that it would be a big thing to start Opening Day. And let's face it, a lot of times, when you're the number-one guy, they're counting on you. Guys are telling you, "Hey, man, you're the guy we're counting on. When things get tough, you're the guy we're counting on to make sure it doesn't stay tough or doesn't get even tougher." That's what being the number-one guy is all about. Brett says they have number one and number one-A. I think that might be the case.

MARCH 2, 2008

TAMPA, Florida—Making his first Grapefruit League start, Cole Hamels got roughed up today by the New York Yankees. He allowed four runs, including homers by Jason Giambi and Jason Lane, in two innings at Legends Field.

But that's not what left him so angry.

Hamels has fewer than two full seasons of major league service time, making him ineligible for salary arbitration until at least next year and giving him no leverage in contract discussions. So the Phillies renewed his contract for $500,000 rather than his desired salary of $750,000, a decision they believed was consistent with comparable pitchers of his experience level.

To Hamels, it was an insult.

"It's part of the game when you are in my situation," he said. "You don't have any say. You just have to take it. I just want to see some generosity and understanding about what I'm going out there every five days to do. I just want fair compensation, not the world and the moon. I just want what's fair in this situation. If you are working anywhere and you're doing better than someone else, [and] he's getting paid more, you feel you should be compensated."

Hamels, 24, went 15–5 with a 3.39 ERA in 28 starts last season and is 24–13 with a 3.68 ERA in his career, easily making him the Phils' best starter. But he also missed a month with an elbow strain and hasn't stayed healthy for a full season. And, at similar stages in their careers, after having similar success to Hamels, Dontrelle Willis (24–17, 3.70 ERA, $378,500 in 2005), Scott Kazmir (22–20, 3.73 ERA, $424,000 in 2006), and Chien-Ming Wang (27–11, 3.77 ERA, $489,500 in 2007) each made less than what Hamels will make in 2008.

.   .   .   .

There are different ways to look at it. When you look at Troy Tulowitzki, the shortstop over in Colorado, that organization saw fit to almost secure him with a nice contract. I think that you have to understand your own organization, and I know that Barry Bonds had gone through that. But a lot of times, keep in mind, sometimes players don't forget what they consider to be a slight, and sometimes ownership doesn't forget when a player has a reaction to something. And, sometimes, that's why players go get [high-powered agent] Scott Boras, because they're tired of this or that. But the guys who can play, the guys who can pitch, the guys like Cole Hamels, he'll get his due. He'll get his money. I mean, Cole is a special pitcher. He's got that great change-up, and that's one of the things that makes him so effective. He just has to go out there, stay healthy, and keep pitching the way he's capable of, and if he does that, he'll be fine. Everything else will take care of itself.

MARCH 3, 2008

CLEARWATER, Florida—Every so often—between Ryan Howard's arbitration hearing, Brad Lidge's balky knee, and Cole Hamels's salary complaints—life intervenes and reminds everyone how unimportant baseball can be.

Davey Lopes has prostate cancer.

Lopes, the Phillies' first-base coach, was diagnosed after undergoing his annual physical at spring training, and doctors are optimistic that they caught the cancer early enough for him to make a complete recovery. Lopes, 62, has taken a leave of absence and will undergo surgery in two weeks at Morton Plant Hospital in New Port Richey, Florida.

"It's unfortunate, but fortunate," said pitcher Jamie Moyer, who works with cancer patients and their families through his charitable work. "It's fortunate that we do physicals, and it's early enough to catch something like that. Hopefully, it was caught in time. It sounds like it was detected early, they'll knock it out, and life will go on. Hopefully, it can be a positive story."

Former Phillies outfielder Jerry Martin, a minor league instructor, will coach first base while Lopes is being treated. Charlie Manuel said Lopes likely will miss four to six weeks.

·   ·   ·   ·

Davey is a class act. He's tough as nails. He didn't want people to know, really, and he doesn't want sympathy. He doesn't want to come back until he can do his job, plain and simple. That doesn't surprise me, though. That's why we didn't like him when we were playing against him. We knew what kind of character he had. Everybody's worried until you get the word that it's gone, that it's not there anymore. No one takes anything for granted when it comes to that, you know. That doesn't just go with Davey, but other friends who have gone through cancer, too. From Bobby Murcer, along with Vuke [late Phillies player/coach John Vukovich, who passed away last year after battling a brain tumor]. Shoot, it's scary. Nobody wants to think about anything like that, and when it happens, yeah, it's scary. With Davey, hopefully they caught it early enough, and he can get well and get back on the field where he belongs.

MARCH 15, 2008

CLEARWATER, Florida—Everyone, it seems, has a Pat Gillick story.

John Olerud, the former All-Star first baseman, talks about the nine trips Gillick made to watch him play at Washington State University before signing him with the Toronto Blue Jays. Colleagues marvel at his knack for memorizing phone numbers (Earl Weaver once nicknamed him "Wolley Segap," Yellow Pages backward). When he considered signing reliever Gregg Olson for the Blue Jays in 1994, he didn't wait for the free-agent to have his injured elbow examined. Instead, he found out which flight Olson was taking to see Dr. James Andrews in Birmingham, Alabama, and booked the seat next to him.

And after flying to Kansas City to talk free-agent outfielder Joe Carter into re-signing with the Blue Jays in November 1992, Gillick told team president Paul Beeston that he wanted to make an unscheduled stop in Milwaukee on the way home.

"For what?" Beeston asked.

"Dinner with [Paul] Molitor," Gillick said.

"For what?" Beeston repeated, incredulously. "It's the night before Thanksgiving."

But Gillick was insistent. They met with Carter, then hopped a flight for a pre-turkey dinner with Molitor and his agent, Ron Simon. Two weeks later, on the day Carter decided to stay with the Blue Jays for five more years, Molitor left Milwaukee after 15 seasons and accepted a three-year, $13 million offer from Toronto.

"The rest of the United States took the day off before American Thanksgiving," Beeston said, "but not the Toronto Blue Jays and Pat Gillick. He's relentless. That's what sets him apart."

Gillick, 70, plans to step down as the Phillies' general manager when his three-year contract expires after the season. Since he took the job in November 2005, Gillick has made both shrewd moves (trading for Aaron Rowand and Jamie Moyer, claiming Greg Dobbs off waivers, signing Jayson Werth) and awful ones (signing Adam Eaton and Wes Helms).

But he also led the Phillies to the postseason for the first time since 1993. In 26 seasons as a general manager, he has taken four teams to the playoffs (Toronto, Baltimore, Seattle, and the Phillies), and he won World Series rings with the Blue Jays in 1992 and 1993. Gillick is so old-school that he thinks MySpace is the area around his desk, but with a traditional emphasis on scouting, he has left an impression on his Phillies colleagues.

"It's easy to see why he has been so successful," assistant GM Mike Arbuckle said. "His mind is always looking for a new angle, and with his energy level, he's ready to jump into action. He's incredible."

. . . .

He's had a great career. He knows talent. Obviously, there have been some mistakes that have been made. But look at the other clubs. They've made mistakes, too. But look at how much success his clubs have had over the years and how they've emerged. That's another feather in his cap, another notch in his belt, and he's to be commended for that. That's a hell of a thing to do, take four teams to the postseason, win a couple of World Series. He's the one in charge, so he's got to be able to get tremendous praise for what he's done. He's done

Charlie Manuel was all smiles during spring training as his team began their quest for another NL East title.

some great things. I've gotten a chance to know his reputation over the years, being around the game and being around guys who played for him. Then, when I went to Toronto, you heard all about Pat Gillick there. He's obviously revered there for the things he was able to do with those teams.

He's well-known for memorizing phone numbers, things like that. That's him. I can do that, too, you know. I know a couple. But you look at what he's been able to do here, getting guys like Dobbs and Werth. Those were great moves that have really helped the team win. There isn't enough you can say about Pat and the way he evaluates players and understands how they fit with a team. That's the sign of a good general manager.

MARCH 27, 2008

LAKELAND, Florida—The final day of a series, when the team charter is gassed up and ready to fly, is commonly called "getaway day."

Today is the ultimate getaway day.

After seven weeks, even longer for some players, the Phillies finally are leaving Florida to launch their season. During the last days of spring training, Brad Lidge went on the disabled list (he is expected to be back by the season's first weekend), Adam Eaton sewed up the number-five spot in the starting rotation (Chad Durbin will pitch out of the bullpen), and catcher Chris Coste's autobiography, *The 33-Year-Old Rookie*, was released in bookstores.

Mostly, though, the Phillies made final preparations to defend their NL East championship.

"It's a huge opportunity for us," slugger Ryan Howard said. "We've got a really good core nucleus of players. We have a lot of fun as a team. Every year you go out there, you want to win. But you've got to do all you can do while you can. With the business of the game, some guys are here today and gone tomorrow."

•   •   •   •

Defending a championship of any kind isn't easy. For me, coming over here in '81 was great. But coming after the team had won [the World Series], everybody doesn't have that same giddy-up and go that they did previously on trying to win. That's just the way that it is. That's why you appreciate clubs like the Big Red Machine that did it over and over. The Yankees, they fit into that role. The Marlins, only being there five years and winning a world championship, that's great stuff. You have the Cubs that haven't won in 100 years. Like [legendary Cubs broadcaster] Jack Brickhouse said, "Anyone can have a bad century." They've had pretty good teams and been right there a few times. And that's not even winning a World Series. That's just getting there. So you have to appreciate the chances you get. I think this team appreciates that they have an opportunity here. They have a chance to do something special. I think this group of guys knows that.

Chapter 3

Opening Day and April

MARCH 31, 2008

PHILADELPHIA—Used in succession, they are perhaps the finest words in sports.

Opening Day.

On Opening Day, the mercury doesn't always rise after a long winter, and the sun doesn't always peek through the clouds. But with the first crack of a bat and pop of a mitt, everyone, regardless of age or circumstance, becomes a kid again.

Today is Opening Day at Citizens Bank Park.

For the first time since 1994, the Phils will open a season as defending champions of the National League East when they host the Washington Nationals. With a nucleus that includes back-to-back league MVPs Ryan Howard and Jimmy Rollins, All-Star second baseman Chase Utley, and ace lefty Cole Hamels, expectations for them to repeat are even higher than a math whiz can count.

The 2008 home opener was spoiled by the Washington Nationals, who beat the Phillies 11–6. *Photo courtesy of Getty Images.*

Opening Day counts the same as the other 161 games, but it's hardly any other game. The season opener, with its pomp and pageantry, has extra meaning for players looking to make a positive first impression on fans who have been waiting since October to see them.

"I think we're really good. I really do," says pitcher Brett Myers, who will unleash the first pitch at approximately 3:05 PM. "We proved that last year, and we got better this off-season. I think we're a lot better, for sure. It's going to be successful if we win the division again, but we want to go further than that."

The journey begins today.

. . . .

I think the very first one was special in '73. After that, it was like you're going to work. You do the same thing every year. Sure, you have butterflies. But after the first one, you just get after it. After that, you're expected to be there. If you're hitting in the three, four, or five spot, you've got other things to worry about besides Opening Day. And with the Big Red Machine in your division, you're just hoping you're playing back far enough where you aren't going to get injured by all those balls that are going to be hit hard at you. Speaking personally, my most joyous time on Opening Day will be probably, besides Junior playing in the World Series one day, when one of my grandsons plays Opening Day and being there to see that. That would be a thrill. But now, Junior has been in a couple of Opening Days. I played in it all of my career.

I'll never forget the first one in '73. It was great. Willie McCovey, my idol, was in the lineup. I had a lot to live up to. It was the year Mike Schmidt broke in, along with Bill Madlock and those guys. I had Rookie of the Year on my mind. Late in the season, like Mike told me, the only reason I won it is that he had too many strikeouts and I was hitting .300. I said, "Well, good." But after that year, after winning Rookie of the Year, I went to the Dominican to play winter ball, and I didn't like it. I didn't follow it up with a tremendous year, but I still hit .287. It was respectable. It wasn't like .200. But the guys these days, look at Ryan [Howard], the way he followed up his rookie campaign with an MVP award. Look at [Ryan] Braun. I mean, my God. Braun will be talking about guys like [Rockies shortstop Troy] Tulowitzki and [Hunter] Pence in Houston. Those guys are pretty much right there with each other for Rookie of the Year. But that's really what you remember. You remember that first Opening Day and the butterflies that you feel. I think everyone feels that.

.   .   .   .

Opening Day 2008 didn't go so well for the Phillies.

Tied 6–6 in the top of the ninth inning, veteran reliever Tom Gordon, filling in for injured closer Brad Lidge, allowed five runs on RBI doubles by Nick Johnson, Paul Lo Duca, Ronnie Belliard, and Dmitri Young. In the drizzle, the Phillies lost 11–6, drawing boos from a sellout crowd of 44,553. And after the game, they acquired veteran reliever Rudy Seanez off waivers from the Los Angeles Dodgers to help fortify their bullpen.

APRIL 6, 2008

CINCINNATI—It was hardly the circumstance he had dreamed about, trailing the Reds by six runs in the eighth inning. But closer Brad Lidge made his Phillies debut here today, and it couldn't have gone any better.

Lidge, who underwent arthroscopic knee surgery February 25 and was activated from the disabled list two days ago, retired the side, unleashing a fastball in the mid-90s and a nasty slider. He got Jeff Keppinger to line to right field and struck out Ken Griffey Jr. on a slider in the dirt before Brandon Phillips popped to shortstop.

"I felt great," Lidge said after the Phillies' 8–2 loss, their fourth defeat in six games. "I wish it was a different situation. But I was happy finally to pitch in a game and get outs for our team. That's the most important thing."

.   .   .   .

For them to go in there and clean up his knee and have him start the season when he did, who knows, maybe it might have been a blessing. His control was very good, and I think that's because he's not sure his fastball will be there right away. That's pretty smart of him. He's a smart pitcher, and he has great stuff. You just have to know that if he's able to keep pitching well, it's a big thing for this team.

APRIL 8, 2008

NEW YORK—Last year, Jimmy Rollins became a King Kong–sized villain in the Big Apple and stoked the dormant Phillies-Mets rivalry with his notorious "team to beat" comments. Then he delivered an MVP season, saving his best performances for games against the Mets.

So, naturally, with the Phillies visiting the Mets today in the 45th and final home opener at soon-to-be-demolished Shea Stadium, Rollins must have another prediction for how 2008 will turn out.

This time, though, he wouldn't bite—or offer any sound bites.

"Write something for me," Rollins said with a grin. "You have my permission. Anyone asks if I said it, I'm like, 'Hey, they wrote it.'"

But nobody could've scripted what happened in the eighth inning.

Standing on second base, Rollins spun awkwardly back to the bag on a fake pick-off throw by Mets reliever Aaron Heilman. A few pitches later, he hobbled around third base and scored on Chase Utley's RBI double, then removed himself from the game. The diagnosis, a high left ankle sprain, tempered the Phillies' excitement from a 5–2 victory that evened their record at 4–4.

After the game, Rollins downplayed the severity of the injury. But ankle sprains don't heal overnight, endangering his streak of 230 consecutive games played, third-longest among active players behind Cleveland's Grady Sizemore (366) and Atlanta's Jeff Francoeur (334).

"We'll see. It feels fine right now," said Rollins, who caught his spike in the dirt as he tried to get back to the base. "I was more worried about my knee popping, but my ankle went. When I first did it, I heard a nice little pop and felt like somebody dropped a lid on my foot. I could've stayed in the game, but it wouldn't have made sense. When you're at 50 percent, I'd rather not be out there. I'll try to get off it as much as I can just to give it a chance not to swell up."

．　．　．　．

Just a freak accident. That was awful because he wasn't even getting a throw back. That was unfortunate. They said it was a severely sprained high ankle, so you don't know. Athletes always try to get back, and for the most part, try to get back too soon. But he's playing a position where he's got to go left to right, he's got to steal bases. He's such a big part of this team. He's their best player. Chase, possibly, would be the best hitter. Ryan [Howard], we know what he can do in terms of hitting the ball out of the ballpark. But J-Roll is the guy who makes everybody go. He kind of proved that last year. Ryan went down. Utley went down. And guess what? They didn't miss a beat. That's hard to do, and they were out for a significant period of time. They don't label that or talk about it, but they know one thing: when J-Roll is on, when he's hitting, they win. Period. He gets triples and homers and clutch hits. Good defensive player. Great range. He's the best player on the team, so you just hope that he can make it back to full speed pretty soon and that he isn't out for any extended period of time.

APRIL 12, 2008

PHILADELPHIA—Another day, another game without Jimmy Rollins.

And another injury for the Phillies.

Now, they don't have Shane Victorino either.

To recap: after suffering a high left ankle sprain Tuesday, Rollins initially was in the lineup Wednesday night in New York. But he took a few cuts in the batting cage, huddled with athletic trainer Scott Sheridan, and decided he couldn't play. His replacement, Eric Bruntlett, committed two errors in an 8–2 loss to the Mets. X-rays were negative, but Rollins didn't start Thursday night either, striking out in a pinch-hit appearance in a 4–3, 12-inning loss to New York.

Then, after returning home and beating the Cubs without Rollins last night, the Phillies won again tonight 7–1 over Chicago. But Victorino, the speedy center fielder who has filled in for Rollins in the leadoff spot, strained his right calf while scoring from third base on a wild pitch and went on the disabled list after the game. Victorino may have been able to avoid the DL, but with Rollins sidelined, the Phillies couldn't afford to have two hobbled players on the bench.

And with Rollins and Victorino out, speed has been drained from the Phillies' lineup. But they have a 6–6 record and are only 1½ games off the Florida Marlins' pace in the NL East because of Chase Utley and Pat Burrell. In 12 games, Utley is

15-for-46 (.326) with three home runs and eight RBIs, while Burrell, a free agent after the season, is 14-for-37 (.378) with four homers and 12 RBIs.

. . . .

You play 162 games. That's why you're not going to luck out in winning the division. It'll show you the caliber of players they have if they're able to win consistently while Rollins and Victorino are out of the lineup. For as long as you can, you've got to keep getting lightning in a bottle from some guys. Pat is doing a great job right now. But if Pat isn't coming back next year, and that certainly has been the talk, regardless, you're going to have to get those 30 bombs that he's probably going to hit from somewhere. Again, I'm a Pat Burrell fan. But I understand reality from the defensive part to the part where you're going to have to pay him, and if he keeps playing like this, his value is only going up. So, if he gets offered whatever amount, even from Kansas City, he would have to go there and play. That's what it's going to boil down to. No one ever speaks about [second baseman Mark] Grudzielanek, but he was one of the reasons we won in Chicago. He's made from the same mold as an Aaron Rowand. Same identical mold. You've got to go to him over and over and over in terms of being a leader. You've got to learn to respect this guy and follow him, and when guys like that go to different clubs, they make those clubs better. They're character guys.

The point is, over the course of a season, you're going to need different guys to step up, and right now, Utley and Pat, they're doing the job. Look, this is a team that can win games in a lot of different ways, with their speed, with their power.

Utley has been showing everyone what he's all about by getting some clutch hits at some very clutch times. Pat has been doing a great job. And they're doing it at a time when the team really needs it, with J-Roll being out and Shane being out.

APRIL 15, 2008

PHILADELPHIA—Growing up in central Florida in the mid-1980s, Tom Gordon lettered in three sports at Avon Park High School. He was a small but quick point guard on the basketball team and had so much success as a tailback that he got a scholarship offer to be Barry Sanders's backup at Oklahoma State University.

But, always, he preferred baseball.

So it pains Gordon that so few African Americans are playing it anymore.

Today marks the 61st anniversary of Jackie Robinson's debut with the Brooklyn Dodgers, becoming the first black player in the majors. But, according to a report released last year by the University of Central Florida, only 100 major leaguers—or 8.4 percent of the total player pool—in 2006 were African American, the lowest percentage in nearly two decades.

"I try to talk to my community about it," said Gordon, whose son, Devaris, recently started playing baseball and is expected to be drafted next month. "The kids say the same two things: 'Baseball's boring,' and, 'You're one of the only black pitchers in the game.' We have to let our kids see that we do have more African Americans in the game.

"That's what we need. We need kids to look at Ryan Howard, to look at Jimmy Rollins, and see that African Americans can play baseball, too. It's sad to see how low the numbers have gotten. It shouldn't be where it is."

It wasn't always like this.

In 1975, when Sarge was in his third full season with the San Francisco Giants, the African American population in the majors reached an all-time high at 27.5 percent. Even as recently as 1995, 19 percent of players were African American.

"I'm disappointed by it," Detroit Tigers pitcher Dontrelle Willis said of the dramatic decline over the past 10 years. "I don't even know what Jackie would say."

· · · ·

In my playing days, there wasn't a day that went by that I didn't think about any of the guys who played before me. It's great that Major League Baseball is bringing it to light each year, that they recognize the day that Jackie Robinson came into the league. More of the guys who play today, like J-Roll, know about that day and talk about it. I think that's great. But in the same instance, when you know and you take on that responsibility as a spokesman, you have to realize that some of the things now that you do might reflect in some ways on how people think about you and the guys who came before you. So, in other words, you think about Jackie and the way that he played—Jackie hustled every minute of every hour that he ever played on the field. And when you're recognizing and giving praise to a guy and knowing that you got your chance because of him, then there shouldn't be a day that you go out there that you don't do those particular things. When you talk to a lot of the Philadelphia Negro League guys, they'll tell you how mean Jackie Robinson was on that field, and for good reason. He really had to be. It's a more polite game today. But, again, when you're looked upon as leader, and people are looking up to you, you have to be really careful not only with what you say but the things that you do on and off the field, because it reflects on so many other people other than just yourself.

It's not disappointing to me at all to see the numbers going down, because a lot of the athletes are doing different things. With the RBI [Reviving Baseball in Inner Cities] Program that Major League Baseball has now, you would think that they're trying to do something about it. But, at the same time, it's not up to me, it's up to other people to think if it's counterproductive when Kenny Lofton doesn't have a job and Barry Bonds doesn't have a job, and you're trying to say that you want more blacks in the game. Certainly, Lofton is an upstanding citizen. And until he's been proved guilty, Barry is the same way. Some guys are able to play it out. Cal [Ripken] was able to play it out. Roger Clemens was able to play it out with circumstances swirling. Again, it's a story that is very sensitive, but it's a story that it's easy to fix just by answering questions (not mine) that the media would ask different organizations about the draft. Where do they go to draft? Have you been to these schools? Have you gone into the inner city?

For guys who are Junior's age, it's an easier way out to play basketball or football. It's the same as it would be in the Latin cultures. Why do they play more baseball than basketball and so on? It's an easier way out. They see their heroes on a daily basis right there on the field on TV. It's the same here in the States. They see the guys—[Allen] Iverson and LeBron [James], you see those guys every day. I mean, you can't tell baseball or an individual club with a free enterprise that they should do this or do that, or market this guy over that guy. A guy like Milton Bradley is going to be out there [as a free agent] after the season. But he has a bad reputation. Let's see how aggressive teams will come at him. He doesn't realize that, "Hey, man, I had a good year. Let me keep my mouth shut and see what happens." What he has done is fall into the same old trap where people are going to say, "I don't want to go near that guy," just because of the statements that he makes. They're not just going to give you the money to give it to you. So, yeah, the numbers [of African American players] have gone down, but there are a lot of reasons for it, and you can't fix it overnight.

APRIL 18, 2008

PHILADELPHIA—As a late-inning reliever, J.C. Romero isn't required to be sitting in the bullpen during the first few innings of a game.

But, tonight, he didn't dawdle.

Romero wanted to watch each pitch thrown by Phillies ace Cole Hamels and his New York Mets counterpart Johan Santana in the opener of a three-game series at Citizens Bank Park. Before the game, Romero said he'd "just be a fan" and joked that he may even bring popcorn to the bullpen to watch the marquee matchup of the National League's top left-handed pitchers.

Santana, at least, didn't disappoint.

While Hamels yielded five runs (four earned) on eight hits and three walks in seven innings, Santana, a two-time Cy Young Award winner and the Mets' new $137.5 million ace, confounded the Phillies' Jimmy Rollins–less lineup by mixing his fastball, slider, and devastating change-up. And although the Phillies (8–9) finally chased him with back-to-back singles to open the eighth, they were unable to complete a comeback against the Mets' bullpen in a 6–4 loss.

"He's someone I've followed the last couple of years," Hamels said of Santana. "When I was in high school and played fantasy baseball, I definitely wanted him on my team because he got me tons of points. Ever since I got into pro ball, he's stayed healthy and put up great numbers, and he's someone I definitely aspire to be."

• • • •

No question, Santana is a great pitcher. But when you deal with a pitcher of that magnitude, you try to have a game plan. And that game plan could change the next time up, depending on the situation and what that guy has going that day. For instance, you might go up there and he doesn't have his control, he's walking a lot of guys, and all of a sudden, now you're able to work the count. It may be a situation where you say, "Okay, guys, let's go after his fastball." He's throwing his fastball, and you're aggressive on it because he's throwing it in the zone, and you're attacking it. So, therefore, those types of pitchers, the Drysdales and the Koufaxes, they have to be considered different. When you think of Santana, you have to go up there with the mindset that, I'm not trying to hit home runs. I'm trying to square up a ball and, early in the count, I want it to be my pitch, which is going to be a fastball because I know when he gets ahead in the count he still can throw his change-up or he'll throw it behind in the count, too. So I always want to try to stay with my strength. I don't want to hit the pitcher's strength. I don't want to give him the upper hand. There's no set way to go about it. Personally, I might think of moving up toward the pitcher because I like to take away that change-up. But he still throws a cutter. If you stand deep in the box, you get the full break on everything. But guys have different philosophies on how they hit and how they attack a guy like Santana.

No matter what, it's not fun. You're not necessarily feeling too good about it. But you're just hoping something happens to where you can get some good at-bats against the guy and put something together. That's how you have to attack a guy like that.

APRIL 20, 2008

PHILADELPHIA—Three days ago, after the Phillies' medical and training staffs reviewed MRI results on Jimmy Rollins's sprained left ankle, assistant general manager Ruben Amaro Jr. assured that the MVP shortstop would not have to go on the disabled list.

Then, today, Rollins went on the 15-day DL.

So what happened?

Rollins admitted before tonight's sweep-averting 5–4 win over the New York Mets that he never thought the injury would linger for this long. But his ankle hasn't responded to treatment, leaving Rollins to concur with athletic trainer Scott Sheridan that the best course of action is to rest it completely.

Problem is, because Rollins pinch-hit in yesterday's game, he isn't eligible to be activated until at least May 5. If he hadn't played, the Phillies could've back-dated the move and activated him sooner.

Oops.

"We had talked through this whole process about whether it made sense for us to DL him [earlier]," Amaro said before Rollins went on the disabled list for the first time in his career. "Jimmy just didn't feel comfortable with that situation. His ankle continued to feel better. It just got to the point where it maxed out. He didn't get to the point where he could play like Jimmy Rollins could play without risking more injury. And we agreed."

.   .   .   .

The thing is, when it happened, you don't know how long it will last. But the fact is, it cost him a lot more time than anybody thought it would. The injury lingered on, and he may not be himself again for a long time. I certainly thought he'd be back sooner because he wasn't put on the DL right away, so you're thinking, "Okay, it's not that bad." But it's one of those things that didn't get better really quick. Athletes always try and get back, and for the most part, they try and get back too soon. But it wouldn't allow him to play. You have to remember that, for J-Roll, his legs are the most important part of his game. He needs to be able to steal bases, go left to right at his position on defense. If he can't do that stuff, he can't really be himself. So you just need for him to get himself healthy and get back on the field.

I'm sure it's tough on him. I'm sure he wants to play. But, no, I really haven't talked to him a lot about it—having gone through injuries myself, realizing in the major leagues that you're either in the party or you're not, you're either playing or you're not. Period. You can do all the talking in the world, but you're either out there or you're not. Sure, guys sympathize with you when you're hurt, but the sympathy really comes from wins and losses. It's a hard fact, but that's just how it goes.

APRIL 21, 2008

DENVER – Chase Utley's daily schedule looks something like this:

- Hit a home run.
- Make a diving catch (or two).
- Save an animal and the environment.

Superheroes aren't this busy.

But Utley did it all tonight in the Phillies' 9–5 victory over the Colorado Rockies at Coors Field. In the third inning, he launched himself in the air, practically getting parallel with the ground, to snatch Clint Barmes's grounder that hit the mound and changed direction. If the ball had gotten past Utley, it almost surely would've scored at least one run, perhaps two, and the Rockies already were leading 3–0 and had the bases loaded with one out.

Then, in the sixth, Utley flashed his short, compact swing and tied a franchise record by joining Dick Allen (1969), Mike Schmidt (1979), and Bobby Abreu (2005) as the only Phillies players to homer in five straight games.

The accolades are pouring in for Utley, who volunteers with his wife at the Philadelphia chapter of the SPCA (Society for the Prevention of Cruelty to Animals) and has advocated to stop global warming. If Charlie Manuel had to pick his baseball Mount Rushmore, he'd start with Kirby Puckett, Harmon Killebrew, and possibly Jim Thome. But he puts Utley's name alongside theirs.

And Utley's college roommate, Rockies third baseman Garrett Atkins, believes he is the early favorite to win the NL MVP Award.

"He's a great hitter," Atkins said, "and when things are going well, like they are right now, anything is possible."

Added Phillies outfielder Geoff Jenkins, "How he plays the game, the way he hustles, he's the best in the game, hands down. If you were to mold a player, you'd start with Chase Utley."

. . . .

The thing you like about Utley right now, he's really been setting up the pitchers and hitting his pitch. Now, some pitchers are going to make some adjustments on him, and in turn, he's going to have to make some adjustments. But the guy is a pure hitter,

Chase Utley helped carry the Phillies' offense after Jimmy Rollins went down with an ankle injury. *Photo courtesy of Getty Images.*

and he has developed a style of hitting that is conducive for his style. In other words, he doesn't always follow through, but when he hits the ball, he's in the same zone as Ted Williams was and other great hitters were. Nothing is slump-proof, but he's in a position that allows him to be able to hit good pitching. When you're in that position, you're able to foul off enough tough pitches to where you can get a cookie and be able to still square it up. The thing about [Ryan] Howard is that pitchers know they can get Howard out, but when they don't, he squares up pitches. And when he does, he's like he is when he won the MVP. Chase has a more consistent approach. He's more of a line-drive type of hitter. He hits the ball hard, but he's not a guy who always elevates the ball like the big home-run hitters do. He's very, very blue-collar. You watch how hard he works in batting practice. He doesn't say much, but he just goes out and does his work. He's just a pure hitter, and he's as good as they get.

APRIL 23, 2008

MILWAUKEE—Pity Clint Hurdle.

Leading 6–5 in the ninth inning last night, and with the Phillies runners on second and third and one out, the Rockies manager was faced with an impossible decision. Either he could have closer Manny Corpas pitch to slumping Ryan Howard or he could have Corpas walk Howard to pitch to sizzling Pat Burrell.

Flip a coin.

Hurdle elected to walk Howard, setting up a potential double play and a righty-on-righty matchup between Burrell and Corpas. Burrell fell behind 0–2, then waited for a fastball and swatted a bases-clearing double that gave the Phillies their third straight victory, 8–6, and at 11–10, they're over .500 in April for the first time since April 18, 2005.

"Usually, that doesn't happen until June," Burrell said.

So the Phillies arrived today in Milwaukee, where Geoff Jenkins played for the past 10 seasons. Jenkins, who took out a full-page ad in the newspaper to thank fans before he signed with the Phillies, got a standing ovation before Prince Fielder's eighth-inning homer gave the Brewers a 5–4 victory. Jenkins is off to a slow start. Splitting time in right field with Jayson Werth, he's batting .239 (16-for-67) with one home run and three RBIs.

·   ·   ·   ·

That was nice to see. He had some very good years in Milwaukee. But for the Phillies, in order for you to see exactly what kind of year this guy can have, he almost has to be playing every day. He has never really been a platoon player, which is a difficult job in itself. One of the reasons Werth seems to flourish at it is because he has done it. Geoff has a lot of moving parts to his swing. When I had him [as the Brewers hitting coach in 2000], I would tell him the same thing. All I know is that you can start wherever you want, like [Julio] Franco did with his bat in the air. All I'm looking at is when you get ready to get to the zone of that ball, if you aren't there the majority of the time in hitting, you're not going to be successful. Early on, he did. He was stronger, quicker. But as you get older, you lose some of that quickness. So you have the opportunity to make adjustments to your approach. You have a chance to work on it and to fix that. If it doesn't work, then you won't have the success. It's as simple as that.

APRIL 27, 2008

PITTSBURGH—Once he finished talking to reporters after today's 5–1 loss to the Pirates at PNC Park, Charlie Manuel had a 10-minute, closed-door meeting with right-hander Brett Myers. At some point, it's highly likely that these three words came out of Manuel's mouth:

What the hell?

And it's a legitimate question.

After allowing four runs on eight hits in five innings today, Myers is 2–2 with a 5.11 ERA in six starts. His fastball, once a consistent 92 to 95 mph, has barely topped 90 mph, and against the Pirates, he threw almost as many cutters (27) as fastballs (37), even though pitching coach Rich Dubee talked to him before the game about scrapping the cutter completely.

Some sobering numbers for Myers:

7.50—His ERA in his last two starts.

10—Home runs he has allowed in 37 innings.

89—The top speed of his fastball against the Pirates, according to Manuel.

But Myers isn't the only underachieving Phillies player. Ryan Howard busted an 0-for-12 slump with a home run last night, yet he's batting only .174 through 26 games, and reigning National League MVP Jimmy Rollins continues to sit on the disabled list with a sprained left ankle.

Through it all, though, the Phillies are 14–12 and have clinched a non-losing April for the first time since 2003, which brings us back to Manuel's initial question.

What the hell?

. . . .

On the contrary, I think you have to look at the things that are going well. Pat and Chase are hitting the ball, and the way they're hitting it, getting clutch hits at big times, they're really carrying them. They've been able to take pressure off the club, from J-Roll not being there and doing his thing. And, keep in mind, Eric Bruntlett has filled in like a champ and gotten some big hits, too. Obviously, you miss Jimmy, and over the long road, you know how important he is. But, the fact of the matter is, Utley and Pat have carried the club and have gotten the ball to Lidge, who is doing his thing after coming back from his injury. So they've been able to overcome adversity late in the season. It says something about their character. Sure, they miss Jimmy, and they'd like to get more from Howard and Myers and whatnot. But they know they have a job to do, and right now, they're going out and doing it. I think it helps that they had a winning April, kind of got that monkey off their backs. So now they don't have to hear about that anymore. And they can look at it and say they'll be getting J-Roll back soon. Ryan is going to come around. Everyone knows that. It's great that they've been able to do what they've done so far, and Chase and Pat are the biggest reasons for that, no doubt about it.

Chapter 4

MAY

MAY 2, 2008

PHILADELPHIA—Aaron Rowand considered plenty of factors—the team, the town, and, surely, the financial security—before he signed a five-year, $60 million contract with the San Francisco Giants in December.

He just never thought about the wristbands.

Had Rowand signed with the Reds, or even the Cardinals, he could've kept the red "Beer-Pong Champ" wristbands that he wore during batting practice each day for the past two seasons with the Phillies. But, with the Giants' black-and-orange ensemble, they didn't match.

"Now, I'm 'The Punisher,'" Rowand said, flashing a set of recently purchased wristbands with the logo of the Marvel Comics character.

New team, same Rowand.

Rowand, the popular former Phillies center fielder, returned to Citizens Bank Park tonight and received a warm ovation from the fans as he walked to the plate to open the second inning. In the tenth, though, the cheers turned to boos when he lined a go-ahead, solo home run to left-center field against J.C. Romero, snapping the lefty reliever's regular-season scoreless streak at 28⅓ innings.

But, a half-inning later, Rowand was trumped by his close friend.

Facing hard-throwing Giants closer Brian Wilson, Pat Burrell worked a three-ball, no-strike count with two out and the tying run on first base. Most hitters would reflexively take a pitch, and, maybe, take their base. But Burrell is leading the NL in RBIs, and Wilson was throwing nothing but hard fastballs. So Burrell swung at and missed the next pitch, then fouled one straight back to bring the count full.

The final pitch, another fastball, landed in the left-field seats, and with that, Burrell gave the Phillies a 6–5 victory in the opener of a three-game series. It was Burrell's third career walk-off homer and first since April 10, 2002. And with his .330 average, nine home runs, and 28 RBIs in 30 games, he has helped carry the Phillies to a 17–13 start. And you have to wonder if Burrell—in the final season of a five-year, $60 million contract—is setting himself up for an even larger payday by putting up career-best numbers.

You have to wonder if he'll be this year's Rowand.

.   .   .   .

No, I wasn't surprised at all to see the fans react that way to Rowand. You have an intelligent fan base here in Philadelphia, and they knew the circumstances. But the applause was really for the way that he actually played here, what he gave to them, what he gave to the team. He played the game the way that Philadelphians like their athletes to play: play hard, get bloody, and do the job. Either one of those, if you don't do it, you're going to get your butt booed, and you'll get really booed if you don't do the latter. When I think of Aaron Rowand, I think "no-nonsense." He'd give his life for the game. No one can deny that. He comes up with clutch hits. He came up with some big home runs last year, some big plays. The one intangible that management a lot of times doesn't look at is heart, and this guy has the heart of a lion. I don't think that you can ever overlook that. I think you realize how much he meant to this ballclub. Does that mean that the club should've paid him $60 million? Absolutely not. But when you get rid of a guy, you hope you can get someone else who can give you the same. That may be the case stat-wise, but heart-wise, it's hard to measure up to what he brought to center field. It's glaring. That's one thing about scouts and people who analyze things. They can't listen to a player's heart or determine how much desire he has. They can go on ability or stats and say this is what he does. But stats don't tell the story. That's why Jamie Moyer still is able to win. He pitches with heart. It doesn't matter what hitter is up there. He doesn't back down.

All the Phillies fans appreciate Aaron Rowand, and that's why he's getting the ovations that he is. Phillies fans are notorious for booing your butt when you come back. It doesn't matter who you are. If you're wearing that other uniform, you're going to get booed. But they didn't do that to Aaron Rowand. They'll do it to Wes Helms. They'll do it to other guys. But they won't do it to Aaron Rowand.

With Pat, this guy's a player. Baseball people recognize that. There are clubs that obviously he can fit with, and the one thing about this guy is that, character-wise, he's able to fit with anybody. He's a quiet guy. He doesn't say much. [Ryne] Sandberg was like that. [Chase] Utley's a pretty quiet guy, for the most part. But they all give you effort in different ways. He's having a great start. Pat's one of my guys. J-Roll [Jimmy Rollins], Ryan [Howard], Utley, you couldn't run this club without those guys, but Pat is playing a big role right now for this team.

MAY 6, 2008

PHOENIX—Ryan Howard judges himself by how he feels at the plate.

The rest of the world has a different standard.

"To me, it's all about seeing the ball and having good at-bats," Howard said today after his name wasn't included in the Phillies' lineup for the second game of a four-game series against the Arizona Diamondbacks and 6'10" lefty Randy Johnson, who is notoriously tough on left-handed hitters. "To everyone else, it's about results. That's how it is in the media and everywhere else."

Howard's unprecedented results in his first 2½ major league seasons—129 homers, 353 RBIs—earned him a landmark arbitration victory and a $10 million salary in 2008. But the results haven't been very good this season. His strikeouts have soared (46 in 118 at-bats), his average has plummeted to .169, and since his game-winning homer last Thursday night against the San Diego Padres, he is 1-for-16 with eight strikeouts.

He even heard boos during the Phillies' homestand last week.

"People see what they want to see," said Howard, facing his locker and fiddling with his cell phone during a terse pregame chat with reporters. "I don't really read the papers. There's a lot of stuff you don't see, other stuff that's going on. I try to do what I can to help the team. Right now, I can't get anything to fall. I'm trying to catch a break."

Ryan Howard's early season struggles led to some fans booing him during a May homestand.

He's still waiting. Howard struck out in a pinch-hitting appearance tonight, and starter Adam Eaton walked Johnson with the bases loaded to help fuel a five-run fourth inning in a 6–4 loss. Could it be that the pressure of living up to his $10 million is weighing on Howard's mind?

. . . .

Well, that's a good question. I haven't asked him about that or anything. But I think there are definitely some guys who think about it, yes. If you're only human, you'd think about the money that you're making and maybe not making and not doing as well. But, again, there are guys who have been playing pretty good and not getting paid as well, like [Jorge] Cantu with the Florida Marlins. I would think there are times when it would bother you, but I don't think it's a thing where you lose a lot of sleep over it. As long as you know you're in the lineup everyday—and that's another reason why the guys respect [manager] Charlie [Manuel] so much. He has been sitting him every now and then, but he'll always explain to him why he's doing this or that. It just makes it easier on the player.

I remember a few weeks ago, when we were in Pittsburgh, I was talking to Ryan's brother. He was saying how, even when he's not hitting, with Ryan in the lineup, it just makes the lineup that much better just because of his presence. What happens is that, late in the ballgame, when you walk that one hitter, now those other three guys are going to get better pitches because they don't want to put more runners on base. But then, if you pitch to Ryan, with any swing, bam, he can hit a three-run or a two-run [homer]. Like Harry [Kalas] reminds me all the time, this kid has done better offensively than just about any player who has ever played the game, power-wise. And that's how they judge a player now, based on home runs and RBIs. Look at Reggie Jackson. When you look at that, and put it in that perspective, it shows you what kind of guy he is and what he means to a team. And when you put this era in perspective, this is an era where it doesn't mean as much to strike out a lot. It just doesn't. The same problems we're talking about with Ryan, you talk about with other guys, too. With Ryan, the bottom line for me is that when he's going really well, he's swinging at more strikes. Right now, the balls that they're getting him out on—well, really, he's getting himself out on—aren't in the strike zone. It seems like he's guessing. A lot of guys today are guess hitters. They don't allow themselves to get a good ball to hit. They're not patient. When Ryan gets back to being patient and swinging at more strikes, he'll be fine. The home runs will come. They'll be there.

MAY 7, 2008

PHOENIX—Upon arriving this week at Chase Field (named for the bank, not the Phillies second baseman), Charlie Manuel has received both email and voicemail messages detailing every move made by MVP shortstop Jimmy Rollins during his injury rehab assignment in Clearwater, Florida.

If Rollins sneezed, Manuel heard about it.

And although Rollins's fill-in, Eric Bruntlett, recently had a 10-game hitting streak, drove in three runs with a home run and a double last night, and doubled home the tying run in tonight's 5–4 victory over the D-backs, Phillies officials are waiting with baited breath until Rollins's sprained left ankle is healthy enough for him to rejoin the team. The plan, for now, is for him to play another extended spring-training game in Clearwater tomorrow before meeting the team in San Francisco and being activated before Friday night's game. Rollins, a Bay Area native, even promised his mother that he'll be ready to play by the weekend.

Surely, that's good news for everyone in the Phillies' clubhouse.

Except, of course, for Bruntlett.

"It definitely has been the longest period of time that I've started," said Bruntlett, who has never started more than 35 games in a season but is 24-for-103

(.233) with two home runs, 11 RBIs, and only one error in relief of Rollins. "It has been nice to go to the same spot every day and just relax and get into that routine of playing."

But Bruntlett also has Northern California roots. He graduated from Stanford with an economics degree, and his wife and daughter live in Santa Rosa. If Rollins is back, they won't have a chance to watch Bruntlett play.

"That's okay," he said. "I've had plenty of games where I've just waved at them from the dugout."

Spoken like a true understudy.

. . . .

Bruntlett has done a nice job, no doubt about it. And it was a tough spot. It's not easy to step in and play for a guy like J-Roll. But it'll be very important to get J-Roll back. He's such a big part of this team, it's not even funny.

In spring training, I talked with him and said, "Hey, you've got a lot of Willie Mays in you. Not because you hit home runs, but because you make the other players better on your team." Realizing that, here's one of the few players who can do other things that can make a team win. It's his whole presence. Once he gets on, all the other players think, "Okay, we're getting ready to score." Certainly, if he hits a double, you're going to score. He has a knack for when things are going bad, he has the knowledge and the ability to take over and maybe turn things around. I'm happy he won the MVP last year because he did all of those things and more. So, yeah, it'll be a big lift to have him back with the team. Huge lift. He's so valuable.

MAY 9, 2008

SAN FRANCISCO—When Jimmy Rollins came to the plate in an extended spring-training game this week, the Yankees' minor league catcher didn't recognize him.

"They let you wear a Rollins jersey?" the young catcher asked.

Playing along, Rollins replied, "Yeah, they say I look like him."

There was no mistaking Rollins tonight at AT&T Park. After the Phillies split a four-game series in Arizona, he met the team in San Francisco, across the Bay from his native Alameda, California. With his parents in attendance, and after 19 days on the disabled list and 31 days after spraining his left ankle, Rollins was activated by the Phillies, went 3-for-5 with three RBIs, and came within a triple of hitting for the cycle in a 7–4 victory over the Giants in the opener of a three-game weekend series.

"It's J-Roll Day by the Bay," cheerful Charlie Manuel said before the game.

Indeed, it was.

After grounding out—but running well—in his first two at-bats, Rollins clocked a two-out, two-run homer in the fifth inning against Giants lefty Pat Misch. In the seventh, he laced a single, and in the eighth, he stroked an RBI double off reliever Keiichi Yabu to open a three-run lead.

So, what didn't he do upon his return?

"Hit a triple," Rollins said with a smile.

"We'll save that for later," Manuel said after the Phillies improved to 21–16. "We don't want him to do too much in one day."

Asked if his ankle is fully healed, Rollins said, "Is anything ever 100 percent? But I don't really have to question it anymore. I'm ready. It doesn't bother me. There's always going to be some tenderness every once in a while."

. . . .

I wasn't so much surprised by the game he had as I would be to see him maintain that. That's what it's all about. The key is, yeah, he came back and did that, but it takes a little time to catch back up to where he should be. Sure, it's great that he started out so well. Sometimes, that's the emotion and the ability to know that you can play. But he's missed so much time. I think it'll take him a little while to be able to catch up. There will be 0-fers in there and some good days, too. It just so happens that the good day came on the first day.

But you can see the impact he had just by being out there. You can see the energy that he brings to the rest of the guys, just by his very presence. He never really was himself for a long time. The injury just lingered on. It didn't get better real quick. But only God knows when he felt good. It's just good to have him back because, like I said the other day, he means so much to this team. You can't say that enough.

MAY 15, 2008

PHILADELPHIA—John Smoltz has his own problems, namely a case of biceps tendinitis that has left him on the disabled list. But as he walked to the bullpen to test his arm today, he stopped and talked to Brett Myers.

Myers, the struggling Phillies right-hander, got hit hard again last night, allowing eight runs (six earned) on nine hits in only 4⅓ innings in an 8–6 loss to the Braves. In nine starts, Myers is 2–4 with a 5.91 ERA, tied for fourth-worst among National League starters. Smoltz, more than most, can relate.

In 2005 Smoltz returned to the Braves' starting rotation after spending four seasons as a closer. And although he won 14 games and pitched in the All-Star Game that year, he described his transition back to starting as "a stinkin' war."

"People don't understand the difference," Smoltz said. "They just assume if you're throwing, you're throwing. As a starter, you better have your A-game almost every time. If you don't have your A-game, you've got to have a darned good B-game. As a closer, you can get by with a B or C performance because you only have to get three outs.

"The thing I can say is my track record, just like [Myers's] track record, was pretty good before the change. I'm pretty sure they'll be pretty good afterwards. There's a big adjustment to be made, and he'll make it. It's not like you're talking about someone who hasn't had success. Mentally and physically, you have to deal with something you haven't done in a while. But he's going to be fine, I'm telling you."

That's what catcher Chris Coste keeps telling Myers.

"He'll be the guy on the mound for the seventh game of the World Series, and we'll laugh about this," Coste said.

. . . .

I know that Brett really liked closing last year. For me, he doesn't have that same swagger that he had when he was closing. He doesn't have that cocky attitude out there on the mound. And there have been times when it doesn't seem like his velocity is there. Whether or not that's because he's throwing too many cutters, I don't know. But Brett knew after they got [Brad] Lidge [in November] that he wasn't going to be the closer here anymore. Maybe it didn't really sink in. I don't know. But I don't know that he even could've done as good a job as Lidge. He's had the experience in this. He's had some great success, but the other thing is, he's had some great failure, too. So, he's not taking anything for granted. Whereas guys that just get in it and have really great success, like [Ryan] Dempster, like Brett, they say, "Shoot, this is easy." But a guy like Smoltz can tell you, when you go through those times, when you're losing and your team needs you in a one-run game, and you let them down, now what's going on? Brett hasn't had the opportunity to ever go through that. If you're a closer long enough, you're going to go through it.

Every player goes through it, those tough times. I think they're taking kind of a tough-love approach with Brett right now. Dallas [Green] did the same thing to us. You weren't hitting? Guess what? Your name was in black print. You want your name out of black print? Hit the ball. Simple as that. Brett just needs to get a few good starts under his belt, start feeling good about himself again.

· · · ·

Two months after being diagnosed with prostate cancer, Davey Lopes has resumed his spot in the first-base coaching box. Doctors caught the cancer early, and Lopes underwent successful surgery March 17.

"Was I scared? Of course I was scared," Lopes said. "I don't know too many people, when they drop the Big C on you, that don't start thinking about things. It was a shock at first. Any time you hear something like that, I don't care who you are, you realize how short a time you really do have on earth."

MAY 16, 2008
PHILADELPHIA—During the past two seasons, there have been glimpses, however brief, of Jayson Werth's power. Usually, they happen in the quiet of batting practice.

"I've seen him hit the ball off the slide in Milwaukee," Ryan Howard said, referring to the mascot Bernie Brewer's perch atop the left-field bleachers. "He hits some crazy balls in batting practice."

Tonight, though, Werth put on a power display for a general audience.

Werth, a tall and lean outfielder, equaled a Phillies record with eight RBIs—accumulated with three home runs—and propelled a 10–3 rout of the Toronto Blue Jays in the opener of a three-game, interleague series on a cold, wet night at Citizens Bank Park.

It was a performance for the ages. Werth became the 18th Phillies player to belt three homers in a game and only the fifth to knock in eight runs, joining Kitty Bransfield (July 11, 1910), Gavvy Cravath (August 8, 1915), Willie "Puddin' Head" Jones (August 20, 1958), and Mike Schmidt (April 17, 1976).

"After the second [homer], I came in and looked at the video, and they put up a graphic," said Werth, a former Blue Jays prospect. "I rewound it and paused it and looked at it and said, 'Man, I have a chance to do something special.'"

It didn't go unnoticed. The waterlogged announced crowd of 36,600 asked Werth to make two curtain calls, and he happily walked to the top step of the dugout and doffed his helmet.

Not bad for a player who would have retired two years ago if not for career-saving surgery on a damaged tendon in his left wrist that was misdiagnosed by the Dodgers' medical staff.

"Who knows where I'd be right now if I didn't get injured?" Werth said. "One thing when I was coming up was I always knew I had power, and I possibly could hit some home runs in the big leagues. Now that I'm healthy, I'm hitting them. Hopefully, they'll continue to come. They say home runs are accidents. I hope I have 20 more accidents."

.　　.　　.　　.

He could have 25 or 30 home runs. He has that kind of power. But a three-homer game, that kind of puts him on the map, doesn't it? That has people thinking this guy here is to be

Jayson Werth acknowledges the fans after hitting a grand slam against Toronto on May 16. Werth hit three home runs and drove in eight runs, equaling a Phillies record.

reckoned with. I felt that way last year that he could play every day. Sincerely, I was saying it, in talking with the coaches, I felt like he could play every day. It's the way he does hit to all fields and plays good defense. He's a big guy. He runs well. And he does things that make the team win. It was no kidding around. I said, "Man, this guy should be playing every day, period." And there were other people who felt that way, too. He might get his opportunity next year if they don't bring Pat [Burrell] back. Even if they do, you certainly think Werth will win one of those jobs, either in left field or right field. He just needs to show he can be more consistent. If he stays off his heels, if he doesn't bail, sure, he can hit right-handed pitching. That's not something you can teach a guy. That's called heart. Does he have the heart to stay in there against a tough right-hander? He's taken criticism for not staying in it. But, for me, he's gotten a lot better with it.

I don't remember him as much in L.A., but I knew he was a good player early on. The Dodgers have had pretty good players throughout their whole existence in the minor leagues. One thing I think that he's showed is he can win some games not just with his offense. You put together a team, no matter how you look at it, you want to have athletes. Certainly, he fits that category. His batting practice is impressive, and he's gotten even better with it. If you look over the past few weeks, a lot of balls he's hitting the other way. When he's hitting that way, he's a tremendous hitter. When he's not going off his heels, he's a good hitter. Again, he's come from a situation where he did start before when he was in L.A. He got lost in the shuffle and got hurt, but due to him working hard and hitting good against left-handers, he kept getting a chance. And now, he's got to make the most of it. You've got to give him a lot of credit for that, you really do.

For me, he has shown the consistency with what he's doing, even now. It's not so much the final product as it is the way he gets to the final product, where he gives you solid at-bats. That's what you're looking for with most hitters. You're looking for hitters to give you a chance to where they're going to allow themselves to get a hit by their approach to the plate. Again, getting the opportunity to play, that's the key. It does something to players when they sit there. It lets them know, "I've got to do better." The more he played, the more you could see we've got to give this guy a chance. Even last year, people were like, "Can this guy play every day? Can he start every day?" The answer is, "Absolutely."

MAY 20, 2008

WASHINGTON—The first lesson came in 2005 on a spring-training field in Arizona.

Greg Dobbs, wide-eyed and fresh-faced and dead set against returning to the minors, arrived at the Seattle Mariners' camp and saw first baseman Richie Sexson and third baseman Adrian Beltre, sluggers who had signed as free agents for a combined $114 million. Dobbs wondered where, exactly, another corner infielder fit into Seattle's plans.

Then he met Dave Hansen.

Hansen had spent the previous 14 seasons in the majors largely because he had mastered the art of pinch-hitting. Need a clutch hit late in a game? Hansen, a left-handed hitter, could provide that service. But pinch-hitting is widely considered the most thankless job in baseball, so Dobbs reached out to Hansen for advice.

Thus began the education of baseball's best pinch-hitter.

Dobbs led the majors with 18 pinch-hit RBIs for the Phillies last season, and so far this year, his production in a pinch has reached ridiculous heights. Including the ninth-inning single that he lobbed into center field here tonight to score pinch-running Eric Bruntlett and give the Phillies a 1–0 victory over the Washington Nationals, Dobbs is 10-for-22 with a majors-leading nine RBIs as a pinch-hitter.

Some perspective: Lenny Harris, the all-time leader with 212 pinch-hits, was a .264 career hitter off the bench and never collected more than 13 pinch-hit RBIs in a season. Hitting in a pinch is never a cinch, unless Dobbs is at the plate.

So, what's his secret?

"Ninety percent of it is your mental state," Dobbs said. "It's being able to stay positive, being able to focus on one at-bat, being able to turn the page no matter what the outcome is. That's the biggest thing I got from Dave. There's already enough pressure. You don't want to make it harder on yourself."

. . . .

I think it's the hardest job in baseball because you're always facing, if not that starter who had great stuff that day, you're facing one of those closers or the setup guy who can be just as tough. They're throwing 98-mph fastballs at you, and you've been on the bench for the whole game. The best guy I saw at it probably was Lenny Harris. On my team, the guy who was really terrific was Thad Bosley. I don't know how many pinch-hits he had in '84 with the Cubs, but it was very special. Very special. He was really great at it, just his approach to it. When I got to the American League, guys went to the cage during the game. They would try to keep themselves loose. When Manny Mota was doing it, those guys would just go out and hit. I wouldn't wish it on anyone. You're facing some of the better pitching, and you might get one pitch to hit. That's about all. It's not like playing every day.

It can be a double-edged sword, too. In the back of his mind, Dobbs probably would like to start and see how he would do as a starter. When he pinch-hits, he seems to have better swings. It takes him a swing or two at times. He's grinding it out, but he's been so good at pinch-hitting, you're almost expecting him to get a big hit. It's unfair to him because, again, when you're pinch-hitting, it's like do-or-die. When you know you're going to get some at-bats, you kind of loosen up a little bit more to kind of look for some pitches. You feel good about playing. But then, you get to the point where you feel like, "My God, I need to do something in the game in order to play the next day," and that's like hitting the ball out of the ballpark. So I don't envy guys who have to do it. Again, it's probably the hardest job you can have on a team, and Dobbs really does it so well.

MAY 22, 2008
HOUSTON—Brad Lidge sat beneath the retractable roof of Minute Maid Park, where he emerged in 2004 as a dominant closer, and said something that folks in Houston never thought they would hear.

"Right now," Lidge said, "I'm probably pitching the best of my career."

Impossible? Hardly.

Over two seasons with the Astros, in 2004 and 2005, Lidge leaned on his blazing fastball to record 71 saves, a 2.07 ERA, and 260 strikeouts in 165⅓ innings. But he never commanded his slider like he has this season with the Phillies, and his ability to paint both corners of the plate with precision has made it an even nastier pitch.

Lidge may have benefited from aggravating a right knee injury in spring training and undergoing arthroscopic surgery. He said it forced him to focus on his control because he knew his velocity wouldn't be up to par when the season began.

Lidge's tenure in Houston soured after he allowed a titanic home run to Albert Pujols in the 2005 NL Championship Series. The Astros survived and advanced to the World Series, but Lidge's ERA ballooned to 5.28 in 2006. Last year, he lost his closer job in April after blowing one save during the season's first week. Lidge was dealt to the Phillies in November as part of a massive roster overhaul by new Astros general manager Ed Wade.

"I really do feel like I'm pitching better," Lidge told the disbelieving Houston press corps before the Phillies opened a four-game series against the Astros. "My arm strength is still there. The stuff is still there. But my control is better."

Then, Lidge improved to 12-for-12 in save opportunities and lowered his ERA to 0.43 by tossing a scoreless ninth inning tonight. For the final out, he threw a first-pitch fastball to the outer half of the plate and got close friend and former teammate Lance Berkman to pop out, securing a 7–5 win powered by Ryan Howard (3-for-5, one home run, two RBIs).

.   .   .   .

When I was coaching with the Cubs, he was lights-out whenever he came in to see us. To me, nothing has changed. One thing that changed with him was when he gave up the home run [to Pujols] in the playoffs. All he needed to do, basically, was to get back his confidence. He didn't come off where he had an arm problem. He came off of things happening to him on the field where maybe he was a little afraid to throw his fastball. That's a tough job. Sure, you want to be good, but realize that no one is good every single time out. Look at the closer with the Angels, [Francisco] Rodriguez. He's saving a ton of games, but he's messed up a few, too.

With Lidge, you wanted to pick out one pitch you were going to hit, which was going to be that fastball. We had professional hitters in Chicago with [Moises] Alou and Aramis [Ramirez], so you didn't worry about them too much because they were going to get a solid at-bat, especially Alou. It didn't matter which guy was out there pitching. They were going to have a solid at-bat. But Lidge saved his share of games against us, there's no doubt. He's got a good slider. It's very difficult to hit. The fastball was the one that Pujols hit out, which would be an easier pitch to hit. That's just the way it is. He might get them out, but our hitters were always looking for the fastball. They were disciplined enough to lay off the breaking ball, especially Alou, Ramirez, Derrek Lee. They weren't swinging just to be swinging. A lot of times a younger kid will do that because they feel like they have to get it started. But when Lidge has his really good stuff, and throwing that slider, he's just about impossible to hit.

MAY 25, 2008

HOUSTON—Five nights ago, after Cole Hamels threw seven shutout innings against the Washington Nationals, Charlie Manuel asked a sensible question.

"Is he going for Hershiser's record?" he said, referring to Orel Hershiser's 59 consecutive scoreless innings for the Los Angeles Dodgers in 1988.

Hamels took a 19-inning scoreless streak into today's series finale here against the Astros. And, after last night, there was no pitcher the Phillies would have preferred to take the ball. Trailing by a run with the bases loaded in the ninth inning, Shane Victorino skied a ball to left fielder Darin Erstad, who threw out Pedro Feliz at home plate for the final out.

In 10 starts, Hamels has a 2.61 ERA and ranks among the league leaders in innings (72⅓) and strikeouts (65). But he could sue for lack of support. He has only five wins, mainly because the Phillies haven't provided him with much offense. He lost a 1–0 decision April 2 against the Nationals and took a no-decision last week in the Phils' 1–0 victory at Washington.

For a change, though, it was the offense that bailed out Hamels. The Astros took advantage of Hamels's flat fastball and rang up six runs in four innings, Hamels's shortest start since September 18 when his still-healing elbow left him on a pitch count. For the second time in 62 career starts, he didn't strike out a batter, and he failed to last six innings for the first time this season. But the Phillies (28–24) reached a season-high offensive output and routed the Astros 15–6 to achieve a split of the four-game series.

"All of us have been waiting for the offensive power and potential that we do have," Hamels said. "We have guys that are going to put the ball in play and get a lot of hits, and fortunately, they were able to do that and turn the game around for us."

．　．　．　．

Cole probably could have a few more wins, but the thing you really like about him is he doesn't put the blame on anyone. He goes out and, at a young age, obviously, he wants to win. But he goes out and puts the team in a position to be able to win. I think having Jamie Moyer on the team has helped him. Cole has done a great job with that so far this year, and you can see, he's definitely becoming a legit ace of the staff.

His change-up has to be right there with [Mets ace Johan] Santana. Early on, his first year, he was getting a lot of strikeouts with change-ups. Santana has had a little more success because he's been pitching longer. But Cole Hamels is nothing to sneeze at. His arm motion on his pitches, it's the same on his change-up as it would be on his fastball. That makes it difficult for hitters to hit. When I see hitters like [the Mets'] Carlos Delgado staying on him, that tells me Delgado has something that Hamels is throwing to give away his pitches. But you don't see that very often. It's very difficult to pick up on that change-up, and that's what makes him so tough.

MAY 31, 2008

PHILADELPHIA—Upon returning home this week, Charlie Manuel noticed the summer-like weather, the soft breeze blowing out of Citizens Bank Park, and proclaimed it "hittin' season."

No kidding. For the past two weeks, the Phillies' run totals have soared even higher than gas prices. On May 21 in Washington, they pounded out 12 runs on 15 hits. Four days later, they piled up 15 runs on 16 hits in Houston. On May 26, they blitzed Colorado for 20 runs, the most they had scored in a game since July 3, 1999, in a 21–8 win over the Chicago Cubs.

And last night they reached double digits once again with a 12–3 giggler over the upstart Florida Marlins, moving the Phillies (32–24) into first place in the National League East.

Over the past nine games, the Phils are batting .324 (108-for-333) with 26 doubles and 18 homers and have scored 85 runs, an average of 9.44 per game. With 41 homers this month, they have set a franchise record for May, breaking the previous mark of 39 in 2006. And for the first time since May 14 through May 19, 2004, they have scored six runs or more in five straight games. Shane Victorino has a career-high 11-game hitting streak. Chase Utley is leading the majors with 18 homers. Ryan Howard has 10 home runs in May, one fewer than the entire Royals team.

So, can this offense be stopped?

. . . .

It sure doesn't seem that way. Everything they're hitting is in the hole. They're having good at-bats. But this is a humbling game. It can get to where you almost don't have any hits. That's why you take it and you ride it out when you're winning and getting hits. It's just a matter of time before some bad stuff could happen. One day the guys could be getting 20 hits, and then they go through a couple games without hitting the ball. That's when you start hitting balls right at people. You're going to have slumps through the course of the season. You just hope you don't have a lot. Or you hope that guys don't go into them all at the same time. Usually, you don't go through the whole season unscathed. Right now, they're in a pretty good rhythm. But you're going to have slumps during the course of the season.

Chapter 5

JUNE

JUNE 1, 2008

PHILADELPHIA—Two weeks ago, while he watched the Preakness Stakes, Charlie Manuel had a vision.

"I'd like to be Big Brown," the Phils' manager says, referring to the champion thoroughbred in both the Kentucky Derby and the Preakness. "I'd like to look back and see somebody far behind. That'd be good."

To clarify: Manuel doesn't want to be reincarnated as a horse. But he would like the Phillies to seize first place in the National League East, build a cushy lead, and maintain it through the summer, the baseball equivalent of galloping away from the field. It might happen, too.

The Phillies moved into first place two nights ago by pummeling the upstart Florida Marlins 12–3 in the opener of a three-game series at Citizens

Bank Park. And after losing last night, they reclaimed the division lead with a 7–5 victory today, as Jamie Moyer improved to 8–0 against the Fish in his career. This time, though, he needed help from Geoff Jenkins and, less directly, from Manuel, too.

Trailing 5–3 with two outs in the sixth, Manuel could've called upon pinch-hitting specialist Greg Dobbs to hit against right-hander Doug Waechter. Instead, a "gut feeling" led him to opt for Jenkins, who smoked a fastball into the right-field seats to tie the game.

When you're hot, you're hot, and the Phillies (33–25) are sizzling. They've won six of their last seven games and nine of 12, and now they have an opportunity to put distance between themselves and the rest of the field.

Just like Big Brown.

• • • •

But let me tell you something: this Florida ballclub scares me because they knock the heck out of the ball when they play against us. Even when we win some of these games, we feel like we lose because they're right on our heels. This young club, before the season, it looked like they were going nowhere because [Miguel] Cabrera's not there, Dontrelle Willis is not there. You're thinking that it should be a little easier. Shoot, it's harder. It's been harder to beat them. [Jorge] Cantu has stepped in admirably at third base after they traded Cabrera, and their pitching is unreal. When we go down there, it's like going out to the West Coast. It's that same feeling. You say, "Okay, we're going out to the West Coast. If we can split, that would be great." That's how you feel when you go down there to play this Florida ballclub.

But, certainly, the way the guys are playing, you could see them doing some things. Being down there by the cage, listening to them talk, it's great. It's like, "How many runs are we going to score tonight?" You know there are going to be tough times offensively. But it seems almost impossible for the team to go into a slump where nobody's hitting the ball the way they should. When they hit like this, you take it for granted.

JUNE 2, 2008

PHILADELPHIA—Years from now, when Jamie Moyer thinks of Ken Griffey Jr., he will remember the sweet left-handed swing, the titanic home runs, the breathtaking running catches, and the bulls-eye throws from center field.

Mostly, though, he'll think of the smile.

"He has always been a fun-loving guy, a happy guy," says Moyer, who teamed with Griffey with the Seattle Mariners from July 1996 through February 2000. "I got to be friends with the guy. I really enjoyed what he brought to a team, his presence. Even as he grew in his career, it never looked like it got tiresome for him."

Griffey, 38, arrives at Citizens Bank Park tonight needing one home run to become just the sixth player ever to hit 600. He isn't in the Cincinnati Reds' lineup for the opener of a four-game series against the Phillies because of what he's calling "general soreness," a mystery malady that is presumed to be a balky knee. But that didn't stop him from holding an impromptu chat with about a dozen reporters for nearly 30 minutes about being on the verge of number 600.

"My dad was always the guy I wanted to be like, and he had a pretty good career," Griffey says from the Reds' clubhouse. "That's the guy who looked like me, acted like me, took care of me. He said I'd be better than him, and I was like, 'Yeah, right.' I was 14 at the time. Sometimes, dad does know best."

. . . .

I knew that little crumb-snatcher, of course. Talking to him, I've told him that I remember when his dad used to have him at games against us at Riverfront [Stadium in Cincinnati]. I remember Barry Bonds running around, too. But you never know the kids are going to be the players that they are. They grow up, and there they are. I remember back to when we were still playing, and Mike [Schmidt] saying that hitting 500 home runs would be nothing one day. Sure enough, look how many guys there are at 500 now. Six-hundred, now that's a lot of home runs to hit in one's career, and 600 for a guy that's had a ton of injuries in the last five, six, seven years. You'd think he would've gotten there a few years ago, but he just couldn't stay in the lineup. It's a great accomplishment. He's been just a great player for the game and for the cities that he's played in. It didn't go well in Cincinnati because of the injuries, which is too bad because it's his hometown. But it damn sure went well for him all those years in Seattle.

It's history. I would love to see him do it here and us win the ballgame. You wouldn't want him to do it when he has a chance to beat you. But it's a hell of a feat, a hell of a feat.

JUNE 5, 2008

PHILADELPHIA—When he agreed to a two-year contract extension last October, Charlie Manuel explained that a manager's power is linked to his job security. He said that a lame-duck manager who frets over his future isn't able to exert as much authority as a manager with the backing of a long-term deal.

Jimmy Rollins was benched by manager Charlie Manuel after he failed to hustle on a pop fly against the Reds. *Photo courtesy of Getty Images.*

Manuel certainly flexed his might today.

In the third inning of the series finale against the Reds, Jimmy Rollins jogged to first base on a pop fly that backpedaling shortstop Paul Janish dropped in shallow left field. One inning later, Manuel benched Rollins, replacing him with utility infielder Eric Bruntlett. Manuel has two rules—hustle and be on time—and Rollins had broken one of them.

Simple, right?

Well, not exactly. Rollins is the reigning National League MVP and the Phillies' most vocal leader. It takes a self-assured manager to bench a player who wields so much clout, but Manuel left no doubt that he has complete command of the clubhouse. After the game, he met privately with Rollins and declined to talk about specifics with reporters, diffusing a potentially volatile situation.

"It's my fault," Rollins says. "I can't get mad at him. That's like breaking the law and getting mad that the police show up. We talked about it before. He's been here four years, and he's told me maybe twice. So, three strikes and you're out, I guess."

Meanwhile, Ken Griffey Jr. remains stuck on 599 homers. He finally returned to the Reds' lineup and went 1-for-4 with a double, as the Phillies (36–26) won 5–0 and extended their NL East lead to 2½ games.

· · · ·

Going through things with one of the best players on the team can be very difficult because the players are looking. They're looking to see, how is Charlie going to handle this? When Charlie spoke up, it was like, okay, he's in control here. That's why they like Charlie. Because it doesn't matter who you are. Not only that, he sticks up for players. He's the one that believes in them. Like with Ryan Howard, people were saying, "Sit him down a day." But he has stuck with him. Regardless of whether Jimmy was right or wrong, it shows you the kind of respect he has for Charlie with what he said after the fact. He said Charlie was right. He said he made a mistake. He broke the rule. He paid his penalty. Period. End of story.

I don't think it was a dangerous situation only because I see the way players play for Charlie. And, besides that, the things they say. At one particular point or another, he's probably had to get on each and every one of them, in terms of the super-stars and the guys that really make the team go. He hasn't backed down from any confrontation, including last year with [WIP-610 sportstalk radio host] Howard Eskin when things weren't going so good. He handles things in the clubhouse. He keeps it in-house. These guys have a tremendous amount of respect for each other.

JUNE 6, 2008

ATLANTA—As Tom "Flash" Gordon stepped off the elevator at the Phillies' hotel here last night, he got a text message from a friend.

Gordon's son had been drafted by the Los Angeles Dodgers.

"Right when I got the news, I hugged Mad Dog [reliever Ryan Madson]," says Gordon, the Phillies' veteran eighth-inning reliever. "I came out of my room, and he was the first person I saw, so we both started hugging. I think for a good 30 to 40 minutes, I just couldn't calm down."

Devaris Strange-Gordon, an 18-year-old shortstop, was selected in the fourth round (127th overall), two rounds earlier than the Kansas City Royals picked his father in 1986, despite not playing baseball until his senior year of high school and being academically ineligible to play this season at Seminole Community College in central Florida.

But through the connections Gordon has made throughout his 20-year major league career, Devaris worked out for at least eight teams over the past eight months. Last week, one National League executive told the *Wilmington News Journal* that Devaris would be drafted within the first 10 rounds.

"I wasn't absolutely sure," Gordon says. "I knew his talent, how far he'd come, and with his character being tested, what type of person he was. But that doesn't get you drafted. What was important was that these teams counted on my word, and when they got a chance to see him at their camps, they saw it for themselves."

The Phillies (37–26) edged the Braves 4–3 in 10 innings, in the series opener at Turner Field tonight when center fielder Shane Victorino threw out the possible tying run at the plate for the final out. It was an ending so improbable that closer Brad Lidge mused, "The force was with us." But hearing about Gordon's son made Sarge, a first-round draft pick (17th overall) of the San Francisco Giants in 1968, think about June 1993 when his son, Gary Jr., was selected by the San Diego Padres in the 13th round.

. . . .

Flash said his son reminds him a lot of Junior, being very thin and needing to mature physically. But it's a long road. There are times when being the son of a guy who played in the big leagues can work to your advantage or disadvantage. A lot of times they're going to expect you to do even more. That's the bad thing. But the good thing is that a lot of times you get a better opportunity because they'll give you the benefit of the doubt because of your genes, so to speak.

When Junior was drafted, it was great, to tell you the truth. The thing is, again, you know it takes a while for those guys to get there. I thought Junior should've went back into the draft. He was drafted by San Diego. He had gone to junior college at Mission College [in Sylmar, California], made All-American. San Diego got him on a draft-and-follow. If he had gone back in the draft, he would've been a higher draft choice. After he got [to the Padres], he ended up being the best player in their organization and called and said, "Dad, you know, I should've waited." But he wanted to sign, so I elected to let him go. I've always allowed all of the boys to make their own decisions. I give them my input. I was strong on that, saying that he should wait and go back [in the draft]. But, again, he wanted to sign.

For me, back in '68, growing up [in Los Angeles County], we had Doug DeCinces and Tim Foli in our area. Foli was actually number one [overall] to the Mets. So, I wasn't really in awe of the draft. There were people in my area who played. Buddy Bradford, for one, who was with the White Sox, was my next-door neighbor. This was like our dream coming up the whole time. I was surprised I wasn't drafted by the Dodgers, to tell you the truth. But it was an exciting time, without a doubt.

JUNE 9, 2008

MIAMI GARDENS—After yesterday's sweep-clinching 6–3 victory over the Atlanta Braves at Turner Field, Ryan Howard made a surprising observation.

"I think our best baseball is still ahead of us," he said.

Really?

The Phillies have won four straight games and 15 of the last 19. They're leading the NL East 3½ games ahead of the Florida Marlins, 6½ ahead of the Braves, and 7½ ahead of the New York Mets. At 39–26, they're a season-high 13 games over .500, and they have their best record through 65 games since 1993 when they went 45–20 en route to a World Series appearance. They are averaging 5.29 runs per game, second-most in the league, and they are allowing 4.12 runs per game, third-fewest in the NL.

If the Phillies' best baseball is ahead of them, it'll be a fun summer.

Thus far, their formula for success is simple: the starting pitchers keep games close enough for the offense to get a lead. Then the shut-down bullpen holds it. It's hardly a novel idea. Over the past 10 years, all the best teams have had the best bullpens, and the Phillies' relievers lead the majors with a 2.58 ERA, 2.35 since April 6.

Brad Lidge is 17-for-17 in save chances with a 0.96 ERA, breaking Al Holland's club record for consecutive saves to open a season and making the trade with Houston last November look like a gem. Tom Gordon has a 2.13 ERA since Opening Day. Left-hander J.C. Romero has a 1.59 ERA in 28 appearances. Converted starter Chad Durbin has a 1.67 ERA in 25 appearances. Ryan Madson has allowed two runs in his last 16 innings. Rudy Seanez has allowed a run in only four of his 19 outings. And Lidge says the Phillies' bullpen is the best he's been a part of, even better than the 2003 Astros bullpen that combined on a six-pitcher no-hitter at Yankee Stadium and featured flame-throwing closer Billy Wagner and setup man Octavio Dotel.

It's hard to argue.

.   .   .   .

The way the offense is going, five, six runs is nothing. You're looking at that on a nightly basis. And when you do that, you're taking pressure off your pitchers. But this is a pretty good bullpen. They feel comfortable that, whenever they have a lead, they're going to be able to keep it. So, to me, psychologically, it does them good, besides the job that the guys are doing. You're up by two runs, you've got Durbin, you've got the lefty [Romero], they're starting to feel good. Now, the concentration is even more on winning.

When you have the guys out there who can pitch, it just makes you feel that you're going to win. Like when Lefty, Steve Carlton, was pitching, we called it "Win Day." That's how good you felt when Lefty was on the mound. That's the way you'd like to be able to feel, where you know that, hey, all we need is two or three runs today. Now, it works the opposite way, too. When they get four or five runs off your starter, or you don't have that shut-down bullpen that you can trust, now you have work to do.

For me, so much of it has to do with the guy in the ninth inning. Everybody always knew that Lidge has a good arm. What he hasn't been tested on is to hear some of the boos in Philadelphia. He's only heard the cheers because he's doing really well. But, believe me, that day is going to come because that's the way the game is. It's a humbling game. As easy as the game is for him right now, you ask him the difference between here and Houston, he'd say there's no difference except for making the pitches that he should've been making. I think, absolutely, he needed a change of scenery. That does wonders for a lot of people, and you see what it's doing for him here.

· · · ·

Meanwhile, the Phillies flew in to South Florida and had a day off before opening a three-game series tomorrow night against the Marlins. Sarge took the opportunity to go to Dolphin Stadium to watch history. In the finale of Florida's series against the Cincinnati Reds, Ken Griffey Jr. finally hit number 600, a two-run shot off left-hander Mark Hendrickson in the first inning. Unfortunately, only 16,003 fans were there to see it, as the Marlins continued to have attendance woes despite their surprising early season success.

· · · ·

Yeah, it was a night off, but I went there for the love of the game, man. Before the game, I went on the field and went over to Griffey. I said, "Man, I sure wish you can do this quick, so I can get out of here." He said, "I'll do it in the first inning," and bam, see you later, he did it in the first inning. I was glad to be there. I really was. It's not often that a guy achieves something like that. It was definitely a special thing to see.

JUNE 12, 2008
MIAMI GARDENS—After dropping the first two games in their series against the Florida Marlins, the Phillies found the perfect elixir tonight to halt their skid and avoid a sweep.

They sent Jamie Moyer to the mound.

At 45, Moyer is the majors' oldest player. But he also is the Marlins' master. In nine career starts against the free-swinging Fish, he's 9–0 with a 3.03 ERA. In four career starts at Dolphin Stadium, he's 4–0 with a 1.30 ERA. And, tonight, he lasted eight innings for the first time since April 19, 2007, and absolutely flummoxed the Marlins. He took a no-hitter into the sixth inning, allowed two singles and a walk, and threw 102 pitches, most exactly where catcher Carlos Ruiz called for them. Moyer has won six of his last seven decisions overall and posted a 3.88 ERA in his last eight starts.

If Moyer knows why he has the Marlins so baffled, he isn't saying. But if the Phils, 40–28 and three games ahead of the upstart Marlins in the National League East, are unable to pull away late in the season, Charlie Manuel surely will figure a way to make sure Moyer pitches against Florida in every remaining series between the clubs.

Actually, he may do even better than that.

"We'll see if we can't get that 45-year-old to throw two out of three," Manuel says. He was joking. We think.

. . . .

It's unreal what Jamie is doing. I'm in awe. Really. His longevity really surprises me just for the fact that he doesn't throw as hard. But he used that to his advantage and got smarter mentally in terms of pitching to major league hitters. Every time the Florida Marlins hitters know he's going to pitch, they break out into a cold sweat. Usually, a guy like Jamie, you would send a limo to make sure he's on time. That's how much you'd want to hit against him. But it's uncanny. They can't beat him.

I never really had a problem with guys like that. Matter of fact, those kinds of days, I always took it like it was a day off. Facing guys from the right side, soft-throwers, it was kind of like Thanksgiving for me. I don't get it, I really don't, when I see the Florida Marlins having so much trouble against Jamie, but it's just that they make poor adjustments. They don't go up and move forward in the batter's box. They don't go and put their hands in the middle of the plate like I would against Randy Jones, Tommy John, those kinds of guys. The problems I had was facing Nolan Ryan or J.R. Richard. Those are the times to take some damn days off. You never did, of course. But a good day against those guys was a couple of punchouts, a couple walks, and then, you kill that lefty [reliever]. It's simple. I mean, you've got to eat sometime, right?

But I'm amazed when I watch Jamie. You look at what he's doing, and that doesn't tell the story on balls that could've been caught. He's pitched even better than what his stats reflect. Not only that, being a leader, doing things the right way, Jamie leads by example, always hustling, always working hard. He's a great

Jamie Moyer continued to defy the odds, pitching effectively for the Phillies at age 45.

example for the younger pitchers on the team, [Cole] Hamels, [Kyle] Kendrick. Why can't he continue to pitch? For me, he can keep going until he isn't effective anymore, and he's showing no signs of that.

JUNE 14, 2008
ST. LOUIS—Last night, in the opener of a three-game weekend series at Busch Stadium, the Phillies pounded the Cardinals 20–2 and sent the historians to the

record book. According to the Elias Sports Bureau, it marked the first time that the Phillies have reached the 20-run mark twice in the same season since 1900.

So leave it to Kyle Lohse today to shut down the unstoppable offense.

Lohse went 3–0 with a 4.72 ERA for the Phillies last season after being acquired before the July 31 trade deadline from the Cincinnati Reds. The Phils wanted to re-sign Lohse, and by his account, he wanted to return. We may never know exactly why negotiations broke down last winter. Lohse contends the Phillies never extended another offer after he declined their first (three years, approximately $21 million). The Phillies insist Lohse's agent, the always aggressive Scott Boras, wasn't receptive to their attempts at further contract discussions.

Draw your own conclusions.

Regardless, Lohse settled for a one-year, $4.25 million deal from the Cardinals, and in his first start against the Phillies (41–29), he allowed two runs on four hits in eight innings and outdueled Adam Eaton in a 3–2 victory. Lohse improved to 8–2 with a 3.77 ERA in 15 starts.

. . . .

He has helped the Cardinals, no doubt about that. His record would tell you that. But let's face it: Lohse got a fair contract. I think, after he looks at it, he'd say that he did. He's jumped out and is having the year that he is, and I think he probably would've had that year with the Phillies, too. Sure, [Cardinals pitching coach Dave] Duncan has had something to do with it. They're to be commended. He and Tony La Russa have done a hell of a job with this ballclub here. But I think Kyle Lohse would've done just great back in Philadelphia, with our ballpark and this team. The thing is, where would he have fit in the rotation? Maybe then Kyle Kendrick wouldn't have been here. And, certainly, Adam Eaton wouldn't have been here as long as he has, providing that he didn't start doing better. But Lohse is a guy who knows how to pitch. He has three quality pitches, and it looks like he has come up with that little two-seamer and also that pitch that backs up on left-handers. He didn't have that last year. He's a good pitcher, no doubt about that.

．　．　．　．

Lohse and the Cardinals got some help from the umpires, too.

With two out in the ninth inning against closer Ryan Franklin, Geoff Jenkins hit a sinking line drive to right field, where Ryan Ludwick dove and appeared to trap the ball between his glove and the turf. But second-base umpire Mike DiMuro, running into the outfield to get a closer look, ruled that Ludwick caught the ball, clinching the Cardinals' victory.

Most of the Phillies personnel—from Jenkins to manager Charlie Manuel to GM Pat Gillick—support the use of instant replay, and last week, Major League Baseball began taking steps to devise a replay system that could be in place by August 1.

But replay is expected to be used only on boundary home-run calls—whether the ball clears a fence, leaves the playing field, hits the foul pole, or is touched by a fan. Other hard-to-judge plays, like close calls at a base or diving catches/traps in the outfield, won't be subject to replay. The concern among baseball officials is that opening replay to other close calls will slow the pace of games that are already too long.

．　．　．　．

Let's face it, on the home-run calls, when it's blatant, sure it would help to have replay. On everything else, all the other calls, if they're thinking about it, I say no. One of the things that makes the game so good is having that umpire there on it deciding whether a guy is safe or not. To have it too mechanical for me just takes away from the whole baseball atmosphere, really.

The ball going out of the ballpark, there are instant runs there. You want to be able to get that call right. With a home run, it's either going to be fair or foul, period. But any time you slow it down on a bang-bang play at first base, it's still very difficult to tell. Do we want to get involved with looking at 10 plays at first base or 10 slides at home plate? Eventually, maybe it will get to that point. You can see that this is just a snowball to see how big it's going to get. I hope that it doesn't. I hope they draw the line right there. During the course of the year, you're going to have a certain number of calls go your way and a certain number go against you. That's the human element of the game. And, no, I never think those calls even out. The ones that go against you always stick out even more.

JUNE 16, 2008

PHILADELPHIA—Seeking to cure a Ryan Howard slump? Send him home.

Going back to St. Louis always seems to bring out the best in Howard. In 12 career games at Busch Stadium, Howard is 18-for-46 (.391) with five home runs and 23 RBIs, and last weekend, he went 6-for-13 with two homers and nine RBIs in a three-game series against the Cardinals.

More impressive, though, were the swings that Howard didn't take. In the eighth inning of a 7–6, 10-inning loss yesterday, he laid off three straight sliders and a low fastball from Cardinals lefty reliever Randy Flores to work a bases-loaded walk and record his fourth RBI of the game.

"It's always encouraging to see him do that," hitting coach Milt Thompson says. "It's got to be frustrating when you're a guy like him and they're not giving you a lot....We've been telling him, 'If they're not going to pitch to you, just take the walk. Eventually, they're going to have to pitch to you.' You have to be patient, but that's not easy."

The Boston Red Sox pitched to Howard tonight, and he went 3-for-5 with two homers and four RBIs in an 8–2 win in the interleague series opener that proved the Phillies (42–30) can go toe-to-toe with the defending World Series champs and left the sellout crowd at Citizens Bank Park dreaming of an October matchup in the World Series. If Howard, who was batting .163 on May 7 and has an alarmingly high strikeout total, can finally get hot, it just might happen.

(Meanwhile, the Mets, mired in mediocrity at 34–35 and 6½ games behind the Phillies, fired manager Willie Randolph after tonight's game against the Angels in Los Angeles.)

.   .   .   .

Some guys do well when they go back to play in their hometown. Some guys, not so good. I went further. I thought any club I was traded from, I wanted to kill 'em and let them know they made a mistake. I don't know if that enters into guys' minds anymore. Too businesslike now, and too many guys changing teams all the time.

For me, the only thing Ryan does wrong is strike out, not hitting for average. The league is set up, though, for his style of hitting—30-plus [homers], 100-plus [RBIs], $15 mil, or whatever. He's got to feel that he's doing it right. In the very beginning of his career, I had problems with the strikeouts. But no one else seems to have problems with them, so I have to learn to go with the age and what's going on in today's game. They don't dwell on the strikeouts nearly as much anymore. In our day, we cringed at striking out even 100 times or so. But, like Ryan says, what's the difference between a strikeout, a groundout, and a flyout? It's still an out. Well, the difference is still a big difference for me. When you strike out, you have no chance. When you put the wood on the ball, at least you have some chance—guy falls down, ball falls in, whatever. But, again, they don't seem to be irritated by it. I see guys who, when they put wood on the ball, [Manny] Ramirez, [David] Ortiz, Jim Thome, it's a little bit different.

Barry [Bonds] learned how to hit. Barry was always a high-average hitter early on. He knew the strike zone. Ryan's problem, to me, is to be a good hitter, you have to know the strike zone. If you know the strike zone, you're not going to swing at a lot of bad pitches. Also, with Barry, you couldn't get him out the same way every single time. For whatever reason, maybe Ryan not being able to pick up the slider as much, he's notorious for swinging at the slider in the dirt. I mean, notorious for it. When he's going well, I don't know if it's being more patient, but for damn sure, he's swinging at more strikes. The balls that they're getting him out on—really, he's getting himself out—are balls that aren't in the zone. It's not just Ryan Howard, either. I think a lot of guys today are guess-hitters. And it's guessing to the point where it's 2–2, they may be sitting on a breaking ball, and they take a fastball right down the middle. It doesn't faze them. I wouldn't be able to sleep for days, taking fastballs. We learned that early on. Billy Williams used to always say, "2–0, 2–1, 3–1, don't be late," meaning, get the bat-head out and look for the fastball. Not enough guys do that these days, and that's why, I think, you see the strikeouts going up.

JUNE 18, 2008

PHILADELPHIA—It had been hyped, this matchup between the reigning champion Boston Red Sox and the upstart Phillies, as a potential World Series preview, a slice of October in the middle of June.

Not so fast.

The Phillies aren't ready yet.

In time, maybe they will be. After three and a half more months, and 88 more games, maybe the Phils will have their starting pitching fortified and their offense in full gear. But after being shut out last night 3–0 by Red Sox lefty Jon Lester and two relievers and battered today 7–4 by the quick-strike Boston offense, they had to settle for one win in the three-game series at Citizens Bank Park.

And the Phillies didn't even have to face Sox aces Josh Beckett and Daisuke Matsuzaka or contend with injured clean-up hitter David Ortiz and first baseman Kevin Youkilis.

But their resolve remains unbroken.

"I still think we match up with them," center fielder Shane Victorino said. "I know we do."

Charlie Manuel added, "This just tells me we've got to play better. That's it. I'd like to see [the Red Sox] again."

For now, though, the Phillies will see another of the American League's top teams, the Los Angeles Angels, in a three-game weekend series beginning tomorrow night, and that means a visit from Sarge's son, Gary Jr. Before the season, "Little

Sarge" lost his everyday job and was relegated to splitting time in the Angels' outfield with starters Garrett Anderson, Torii Hunter, and Vladimir Guerrero. Lately, he's batting .358 (19-for-53) in his last 14 games, but regardless, his pop always gushes with pride.

. . . .

I've seen him so many times, so many of his games over the years, that I honestly don't feel anything other than the fact that you're proud he's in the major leagues and he's accomplished some things that have been good in his career. It's not like I'm really nervous, or nervous for him. Hopefully, he'll get a chance to play. I think he will. But I'm just happy to see he's come as far as he has in his career. When you see him in A-ball or Double A, you never can tell. You're always saying, "Yeah, he has a chance." But there's a lot of kids in the minor leagues, a lot of good players, so you need to separate yourself as much as you can.

It's tough for anybody not to play or to have lost your position because of not hitting. In all fairness to him, with the [hamstring] injury that he has, it's just not allowing him to sit back on his legs the way he should. If that's the case, you've got to be willing to make a change in your approach. You've got to make an adjustment. I don't know if he's done that. He's been DHing. The most important thing is at-bats. It's simple. You've got to hit that ball. You've got to hit to stay in the lineup. You have to be consistent. That's just the way it has to be.

I think he has a lot more pressure because of the fact that, not only did I play in the postseason, I excelled. He has it in the back of his mind. He knows the Angels are going to be there. They have a good lead [in the AL West], and they're a good club. All sons would feel that. I have a friend who does a lot of laser eye surgery. He's always talking about how he inherited his dad's customers, and he's working with their kids and he's taken the company to a new light. But all kids are compared to their dads, whether it's good or bad, whatever sport you play. That's just the way it's going to be, so I'm sure it hasn't always been easy on Junior. I'm sure he feels some pressure to perform.

JUNE 22, 2008

PHILADELPHIA—In the eighth inning today, with four outs separating the Phillies from a three-game sweep by the Los Angeles Angels and a fifth straight loss overall, Shane Victorino strode to the plate, accompanied by Bob Marley lyrics that may as well have become the team postgame mantra:

Baby don't worry, 'bout a thing,
'cause every little thing is gonna be all right.

The Phillies capped their litmus-test homestand with a 3–2 loss and a 1–5 record against the Angels and Boston Red Sox, the American League's best. But as they packed for a nine-game, 11-day road trip, they insisted they aren't concerned about the offensive slump that has gripped the team. The numbers are grim. In the past five games, the Phillies are batting .166—.156 with runners in scoring position—and have left 32 runners on base. In eight games since the 20-run, 21-hit outburst June 13 in St. Louis, they're batting .202—.190 with runners in scoring position—and have stranded 59 runners.

Ryan Howard has three hits in his last 19 at-bats with 10 strikeouts. Pat Burrell is 1-for-19 with eight whiffs. Shane Victorino is 2-for-17. Most worrisome, though, has been Chase Utley, whose third-inning single today broke a career-worst 0-for-24 malaise and prompted a near-standing ovation at Citizens Bank Park.

Utley got a rare day off yesterday, and without getting specific, Charlie Manuel said the All-Star second baseman has been coping with "some bumps and bruises." Utley has dispelled any hint of an injury.

"We seem to be in a rut," Victorino said. "We seem to be in a funk. But we're a good team. We're going to be there in the end."

. . . .

In the beginning of the season, we had Pat hitting the ball very well, Chase was just on fire, and other guys could just chip in. But now, when everybody goes into a slump, when you don't have your [number] three, four, or five guys hitting consistently, you're not going to be able to win. We're not the type of team like, say, Arizona—statistically, the Phillies probably have better stats. But because of those pitchers they have, with [Brandon] Webb and [Dan] Haren, it affords them to not have to score as many runs. So even when they're not hitting, they can shut you down that way. With our particular lineup, and with the staff, you would think they'd have to score four to six runs a night to be successful—on some nights, even more than that—and they're capable of doing that. They've shown that many times.

You don't like it. You don't expect it, but I go back to '83, that happened to us. Joe Morgan never hit the whole year, and you're talking about a guy who won the MVP two or three times. Pete [Rose] was in a slump. [Garry] Maddox wasn't hitting the ball. I led the team hitting .258. When I look back on it, and then I look at this club, I say, "Gosh, this club is even better than what we had."

Athletic-wise, it's debatable, but I think that they're better athletes. But mentally, they're not as tough in terms of the game plan. That's why you can't always go by stats. Stats don't mean anything when you drive in runs when it's 10–1 and you end up with 100 RBIs. It has to count when you're driving in the runs. What kind of key runs? How consistent are you with men in scoring position? Sure, people recognize that. You sacrifice yourself and give yourself up. In today's baseball world, too many times they're trying to get 'em in, not get 'em over. Just about all the organizations complain about guys not having a quality at-bat. Again, it shows you how much they really miss Aaron Rowand. In this game, they shouldn't be able to repeatedly get you out the same way, but you shouldn't be able to hit the ball the same way. In other words, if the pitcher is pounding you in and you're hitting the ball, pretty soon, the pitcher is going to say, "Okay, let me take my chances outside." So there goes an adjustment right there. I don't think the adjustments that are being made in today's game are as rampant as they would be in games that were played earlier. Not to say that all teams don't. Minnesota does a good job of doing that, but they don't always have the talent. The Angels do a damn good job of going first to third. We've seen that over the past few days. They take pride in it. We're looking at what we see in our own division, and we don't see it.

With Utley, for me, there are no excuses. I don't know if he's hurting or whatever. If you're hurt and you can't perform, then you're doing your team a disservice in going out there. If you're able to perform, then you can't say anything. I can't complain that I played in the outfield with torn cartilage and that's why I missed a ball. You don't want to bring that up. And you don't want to bring it up and make it better if I caught the ball with torn cartilage. When you sign up to play between the lines, they expect you to perform. Again, he's just not hitting enough balls hard. If he's hurt and keeping it to himself, maybe that is contributing to that, I don't know. But he's doing the same things every day and going through his training. A lot of his hard-hit balls were actually being caught. Then, he got to the point where he wasn't hitting it hard. Then, he got to the point where the pitchers were making great pitches on him, facing some tough left-handers. All of those things go into it. Same with Pat. You look at the tapes, and boy, they're pitching him tough. They're pitching everyone tough right now. That's just what happens, but the guys have to make the adjustments to counteract that.

JUNE 25, 2008

OAKLAND—One hour before most games, while his teammates are taking extra swings in the batting cage or grabbing a bite to eat, Shane Victorino often watches video of the starting pitcher he is about to face, analyzing his timing and delivery.

It's part of Victorino's pregame checklist, like stretching his legs and loosening his arm.

"I want to know what a guy has going into the game," he says. "If I see something different in the game, I'm going to reanalyze the situation. But if I know what he has ahead of time, it helps a lot."

What, exactly, is Victorino looking for?

It could be anything, really. Any slight movement of the hands, feet, or shoulders can tip him that a pitcher is about to throw to first base or to the plate. It's like a puzzle, or a secret code, and once Victorino solves it, he's off and running.

This is Davey Lopes's influence.

Lopes, the Phillies' first-base coach, reads pitchers like a master thief cracks a safe. Under his tutelage last season, the Phillies had the best stolen-base percentage in

Shane Victorino's speed on the base paths sparked the Phillies offense all season long.

major league history at 87.9 percent (138-for-157). And after racking up three steals tonight in a 4–0 win over the Oakland Athletics, they have swiped 63 bases in 70 attempts this season, a 90 percent success rate. Victorino, Lopes's star pupil, is 19-for-22, and Jimmy Rollins is 17-for-17.

Lately, the Phillies (43–36) have struggled to score, batting .212 with only 31 runs over the past 10 games. So, they've been running more often. They stole two bases against the Angels last Friday and three more last Sunday.

"There's been guys that can run, but they get thrown out a lot," says Lopes, who ranks 25th on the all-time list with 557 steals over his 16-year career from 1972 to 1987. "That's what gives base-stealing a bad name. They don't read. They rely on their God-given speed.

"People say, 'It's an automatic out. I don't want to give myself up.' I know what good base stealing can do. It can demoralize a team. It screws up the best of managers. Trust me, you're not giving yourself up if you know what you're doing."

And that's what Lopes was hired to teach the Phillies.

* * * *

He's one of the best there is in terms of stealing bases. You've got guys who can run, and he can help them be able to reach pitchers. Not only does he do it in a good way by challenging the runners, but he makes sure that before they go, they're reading the same things as he does, as opposed to just giving them the steal sign. I don't know that you can measure that, but you can see the difference in the same guys and what they did before he got there last year. It's not so much how many, but it's the percentage of what the guy steals. There's a lot that goes into it. Knowing the pitcher, knowing the catcher, knowing the situation, knowing whether or not the guy is going to pitch-out, stealing on the right count, hoping it's a breaking ball. All of that goes into it.

He drove everybody crazy because you knew that, if he got on base, the second batter, Bill Russell, not only could take strikes, but he could usually work the ball the other way. They caused a lot of havoc. They played together eight years. That tells you how good they were, really All-Star-type players. They put a lot of pressure on Davey, as the leadoff guy, to get on. But he handled it. He was a great player. Davey was good at it. Vince Coleman was very, very good at stealing bases. Ozzie Smith could steal 'em. Rickey Henderson was in the other league, but obviously, he probably was the best leadoff hitter of all time, with the power and the speed. [Juan] Samuel was fast. But Samuel would've done good or better with a guy like Davey. That's the difference. He could've learned more about how to read the pitcher. Look at Shane. He used to be a fast base runner. Now he's a good base-stealer.

Having Davey around is like a security blanket or some insurance that you're doing things the way that you should. But he's a smart baseball man and a smart base runner, always has been. He always picks up things that most people don't pick up. That's why I thought it was great last year when Charlie put him on his staff.

JUNE 29, 2008
ARLINGTON, Texas—On the February day when Charlie Manuel chose him as the Phillies' opening-day starter, Brett Myers was deferential to ace left-hander Cole Hamels.

"I think I'm a pretty good 1-A," Myers said.

Really?

Two nights ago, Myers got rocked—again—for five runs in two innings of an 8–7 loss to the Texas Rangers. He left the Ballpark in Arlington in a hurry, declining to speak to reporters. But, really, Myers's numbers speak for themselves. He is 3–9 with a 5.84 ERA and has surrendered 24 home runs, more than any pitcher in the majors. Of the pitchers who qualify for the ERA title, the only ones with a higher ERA than Myers are the Dodgers' Brad Penny, San Francisco's Barry Zito (5.91), Seattle's Carlos Silva (5.92), Florida's Mark Hendrickson (5.93), Pittsburgh's Ian Snell (5.99), and Cincinnati's Bronson Arroyo (6.52). And, in perhaps the most telling stat, the Phillies are 4–13 in Myers's starts, including 1–11 in his last 12.

The Phillies remain optimistic that Myers will rebound, but they also lack alternatives. They are reluctant to move surprisingly successful reliever Chad Durbin back into a starting role, while rehabbing right-hander Kris Benson hasn't made a minor league start yet, and top prospect Carlos Carrasco isn't ready for the majors.

Right now, though, Myers is one of many problems facing the Phils. After today's 5–1 loss, they wrapped their interleague schedule with a 4–11 record. Overall, they are 44–39 with a one-game lead in the NL East.

.   .   .   .

I'll tell you what. For next year, for me, after watching him play, I'll tell you one guy I wouldn't hesitate on trying to get, and that's that Milton Bradley. He's got to realize, which he doesn't, that he carries baggage. And if he doesn't, at least the perception of most people is that he's hard to get along with, whether he really is or not. I tend to think he is not, and from talking to a lot of the Texas guys, they say that he's a great guy. But when other people start seeing it—scouts and stuff like that—a guy begins to get a reputation. He might be irritating to you guys [in the media], but he comes to play, he's a good hitter. He's just got to understand that this game went on without Willie Mays. Who cares? But, again, in saying all of that, if they can harness his energy to be able to be on the field, he'd be the ideal player with some energy to bring here to this club. Again, you might need an upgrade in the catching, and you never have enough pitching. But I think Milton Bradley would fit on this team like a glove.

But, clearly, there's a difference over in the American League, and we've seen that. Is it better play over there? I don't think there's any question it's better play. But we got outpitched. We got outhit. A lot of it was against teams in the West—the Angels, Oakland, Texas. There was Boston, of course. Then, there was Toronto [in May]. We see enough of them in spring training, so we know what they're all about. That's a good team, too. Sure, the American League is better. Look at the record. I get that "MLB Extra Innings" TV package, so I know how tough it is. When we're done with our game, we get all the West Coast games, which really helps with doing your homework. So, I knew all about them. They've got some guys in Seattle, when they pitch there, it's like lights-out. Over in the American League, they've got nine hitters that a pitcher's got to face. When a pitcher there wins 20 games, that's a lot better than winning 20 in the National League. They've got my vote.

I could say we just caught some of those teams at the wrong time if we weren't in our own house. The Red Sox and Angels came here, and they kicked ass and took some names, just in case. We were outplayed in every phase of the game. It's been tough because Brett [Myers] hasn't been going well, but it didn't matter. They played National League ball in a National League ballpark and took it to us. The Angels did it. We won the one game against Boston, but then we couldn't get any of their guys out. And, of course, we had our hands full in Oakland. It's always tough to go to the West Coast. It had a lot to do with the pitching over in the American League because the guys were hitting pretty damn good prior to this. A lot had to do with their pitching. They just got outplayed, period. Plain and simple. You can't even sugarcoat it.

Chapter 6

JULY

JULY 1, 2008

ATLANTA—With interleague play mercifully behind them, the Phillies trickle into the visiting clubhouse at Turner Field before the opener of a three-game series against the Braves. As usual, their lockers are labeled by computer-generated nameplates, and their road gray uniforms and blue warm-up shirts are hanging neatly in each stall.

Everything seems normal. But something, someone, is missing.

A few hours ago, unbeknownst even to most of his teammates, Brett Myers agreed to spend three weeks in the minor leagues to regain his fastball velocity and his sagging confidence. The idea, presented to Myers last night by manager Charlie Manuel and pitching coach Rich Dubee, is drastic. And, by virtue of his five-plus seasons of major league service, Myers had a right to refuse the assignment.

But when you own a 3–9 record and 5.84 ERA, and when you have surrendered more home runs (24) than any pitcher in the majors, you're open to any solution, even the most radical.

Last season, Myers grew to love being a closer, a role that he believed gave him "rock-star status." He thrived on the adrenaline rush of emerging from the bullpen to strains of "Lights Out" by California rock band P.O.D. And as he left the Phillies to report to Triple A Lehigh Valley, he admitted that he hadn't readjusted his mind to being a starter.

"This isn't a question of what I want to do. It's what I have to do," Myers said before the Phillies (45–39) won their fifth-straight game over the Braves, 8–3, and Pat Burrell joined Mike Schmidt as the only Phillies players to hit at least 20 homers in eight consecutive seasons. "I need to go work on it, take it seriously, and get back in a starter's mode. That's what I need to work on these next couple weeks, learning to start again."

.   .   .   .

I never experienced anything like that. All I know is any time they said I was going to the minors, even in spring training, it was not a good feeling for me. This guy may have accepted it because it was a relief. Maybe there was some pressure that could be taken off of him. It isn't like he's going to go down and isn't going to get his money. If you say, "You're going to Triple A, and you no longer have a major league contract," well, now you've got some problems.

As far as him still wanting to be a closer, I can't relate to that. That would be like me saying, "Okay, I don't want to start anymore. I want to come off the bench." From all the people I've talked with, you always want to be a starter. A closer is put in a different mold. If they were like a Goose Gossage, okay, then you might understand it because they were pitching 2⅔ [innings]. [John] Smoltz said that he had to prepare himself the whole year that he was going to go starter to closer, and vice versa. Mentally, maybe Brett wasn't as strong. But you've got to be mentally strong when you prepare yourself for 162, whether you're a pitcher or an everyday player. That's the way I was always taught.

Brett just doesn't have the swagger that I saw in him when I got here [last] year. Whether or not that's because he hasn't adjusted to starting again, or because he's throwing too many splits and lost velocity, or whatever, I think it's more confidence than it is stuff. For me, the jury is still out for what kind of pitcher he's going to be for the remainder of the season.

JULY 6, 2008

PHILADELPHIA—It is the most rewarding day of Brad Lidge's career.

And he didn't even throw a pitch.

At an 11:00 AM news conference, before the Sunday matinee against the rival New York Mets, the Phillies announced a three-year, $37.5 million contract extension for Lidge, their lights-out closer. By mid-afternoon, while he sat in the bullpen, Lidge learned he had been picked to make his second career All-Star Game appearance on July 15 at Yankee Stadium.

"I feel like I'm at the top of my game," Lidge said.

No kidding.

By accepting the Phils' contract offer, Lidge forfeited a chance to become a free agent after the season. But while his agent, Rex Gary, predicted that Lidge may have gotten a guaranteed fourth year if he hit the open market, Lidge expressed his desire to stay put.

"I don't know where I could go that would have a team with a better opportunity to get to and to win a World Series," he said. "For me, that's the most important thing, so where better than Philadelphia? This was an easy decision."

So was placing Lidge on the All-Star team. He has a 1.00 ERA and is the only closer in the NL who hasn't blown a save (19-for-19). But he didn't get a save opportunity today. The Phillies (48–41) fell to the Mets 4–2 in a rain-interrupted, 12-inning game, and had their division lead shaved to 2½ games.

· · · ·

That was a smart move, giving Brad a contract extension, don't you think? Rather than having him go another month and nothing happens—then, you've backed yourself into a corner, and he probably goes free agent.

Talking with Brad earlier on in spring training, I wanted to let him know that this really is a special place, and you should feel fortunate to be here. Every time I'd see him, I'd go, "Hey, what do you think about Philadelphia?" He would smile and say he likes it here a lot. For a city to embrace a player so quickly, especially this city, it's uncanny. But they should. Look at the job he's done, going 19-for-19 and not blowing a save.

What he does so well, he can overcome mistakes because he can strike batters out. He gets them to swing at bad pitches quite a bit, so that tells you he has good stuff. He has a live arm, and he's got a good fastball and a tremendous slider. Without him, I'd hate to see where this club would be.

· · · ·

If Lidge was a slam-dunk to make the All-Star team, Chase Utley was a stone-cold lock.

Utley received 3,889,602 votes in the fan balloting, more than any National League player and second overall to only Alex Rodriguez (3,934,581). Utley, anointed as the NL's starting second baseman for a third consecutive season, called the voting experience "surreal."

But not every Phillies player was as popular. Ace left-hander Cole Hamels was snubbed, despite posting nine wins and a 3.22 ERA and leading the league in innings pitched. He also owns the lowest opponents' batting average (.209) and ranks third in strikeouts (110).

And left fielder Pat Burrell will have to wait four days to find out if he will get to make his first career All-Star Game appearance. Burrell is among five players in contention for the final NL roster spot, to be determined by fan voting on the Internet. Milwaukee's Corey Hart, Houston's Carlos Lee, San Francisco's Aaron Rowand, and the Mets' David Wright are also on the ballot.

"I guess I better buy a computer," Burrell joked.

· · · ·

He thought he really was going to make it. The guys are genuinely pulling for him. They really are. He definitely deserves it. But I felt that Pat got jilted. [Ryan] Braun's having a good year, too, in Milwaukee, so he had to be on the team. What do you do? It's a special thing, going to the All-Star Game. It means you're at the top of your game. It's something that every player wants to be able to do, to get recognized that way and do good when you get there.

I think Cole could have made it, and I think he was deserving, too. Although, there it goes with the stats again. If the team had been doing a little better, it wouldn't have even been a question. Pat and Cole both would be there. If they were doing what they should, Cole probably would have another five, six wins, if not more. That probably would've put him in a better position to make it over another guy who maybe has a few more wins.

JULY 7, 2008
PHILADELPHIA—Chase Utley was a touted prospect in 2001 when he agreed to participate in a home-run derby before the Class A Florida State League All-Star Game.
   He got shut out.

Chase Utley participated in the 2008 All-Star Home Run Derby at Yankee Stadium. *Photo courtesy of Getty Images.*

Home-run derbies aren't Utley's style. He is much too serious, too tunnel-visioned, to swing for the fences with the likes of backward-hat-wearing Ken Griffey Jr. or jovial David Ortiz or freakishly strong teammate Ryan Howard. Home-run derbies, Utley says, are for "the big boys," and he doesn't consider himself nearly big enough.

So it was with considerable prodding—"Peer pressure," Howard joked—that Utley agreed today to take part in the All-Star Home Run Derby on July 14 at Yankee Stadium. Utley, who leads the majors with 25 homers and described the event as "a once-in-a-lifetime opportunity," will compete against Florida's Dan Uggla, Houston's Lance Berkman, Milwaukee's Ryan Braun, Cleveland's Grady Sizemore, Tampa Bay's Evan Longoria, Minnesota's Justin Morneau, and Texas's Josh Hamilton.

Critics believe the Derby can foul up a hitter's swing. They point to Bobby Abreu, who won the Derby in 2005 but hit only six home runs after the All-Star break. In 2006 David Wright was the runner-up to Howard, then belted only six post-Derby home runs.

So, Sarge, speaking as a former hitting coach, can the Derby negatively affect a hitter?

· · · ·

Absolutely not. It's one day. It's one round of batting practice. That's it. Guys that are saying, "It's going to mess your stroke up." That's nonsense. I don't buy that. Your stroke is going to come from being mentally tough. There's certain guys who have that home-run stroke and certain guys who don't. Chase is more of a line-drive type of hitter. He hits the ball hard, but he's not a guy who elevates the ball the way that Josh [Hamilton] can. He's going to hit a lot of homers just because of his style of hitting.

But it's definitely an un-Chase-like thing, being in the Derby. He's very, very blue-collar. You don't think of him as a Derby guy. He's more adept at hitting guys who throw hard down-and-in and reading the pitchers. But, in batting practice, you've got to hit the right pitch, right there, and be able to square it up. Chase definitely can do that.

JULY 10, 2008

PHILADELPHIA—For four days, the Phillies' ballgirls and members of the grounds crew have worn "Vote For Pat" T-shirts. Similar reminders have been posted on the left-field scoreboard. And sportstalk radio station WIP enlisted four fans to sit at Harry the K's restaurant in Citizens Bank Park and use their laptops to vote for Pat Burrell until their hands began cramping.

It didn't work.

Burrell learned after today's 4–1 win over the St. Louis Cardinals that he won't be going to Yankee Stadium to play in his first All-Star Game. Milwaukee Brewers outfielder Corey Hart won the online voting for the final National League roster spot, and although MLB didn't release complete results, it's believed that Burrell finished third. New York Mets third baseman David Wright was added as an injury replacement for Chicago Cubs outfielder Alfonso Soriano.

Despite a late push, Ryan Howard also didn't make the All-Star team, marking the first time that a player who is leading his league in home runs and RBIs won't play in the All-Star Game since Hank Sauer in 1948.

. . . .

The way that it ended up happening, you knew Hart was going to get the votes. In Milwaukee, they have nothing else to do but be on the computer for those four days. And then, in New York, you kind of felt David would have the edge just because he was in New York and having a decent year there. But, like I said before, I felt that Pat got jilted, for sure.

I know what Pat has gone through, to have such a good first half and not be able to make it to the All-Star Game. A lot of guys go through that. It happened to me a few times. A lot of times, what you'll do is get off to a better start in the second half to show the fans, the managers, everybody that they made a mistake. Guys today, I think it bothers them but it doesn't linger, whereas with us, it would probably linger on until the next year. It would stay with you a little longer. But I know Pat really wanted to make that All-Star team. He doesn't always show it, but it really would've meant a lot to him.

JULY 14, 2008

NEW YORK—Let's take a break.

After Pat Burrell's three-run home run in the eighth inning yesterday at the Bank fueled a 6–3 win over the Arizona Diamondbacks, the Phillies begin their four-day All-Star break today with a 52–44 record and a half-game lead over the New York Mets in the National League East. And while most of their teammates scattered across the country, Chase Utley and Brad Lidge have come to New York for the 79th annual All-Star Game festivities.

As always, it's about the players. More than 100 of the best, including nearly 50 iconic Hall of Famers, have gathered for tonight's Home Run Derby and tomorrow's All-Star Game. MLB has even scheduled a red-carpet parade through midtown Manhattan tomorrow.

But this year it's more about the place.

Slated for demolition after the season, 85-year-old Yankee Stadium is the star of stars this week. With no indications that the Yankees, a franchise in flux, will return to the postseason for the 14th consecutive season, the All-Star Game may be the hallowed ballpark's final big event.

Everyone has a memory of the Stadium, and Sarge is no exception.

Were it not for a midseason trade to Seattle in 1987, he may never have played beneath the Stadium's famous white frieze façade or in front of its legendary monuments to Babe Ruth, Lou Gehrig, and the others who stand behind the left-center-field wall. But there he was, belting another home run against Tommy John (Sarge batted .385 with four homers and nine RBIs in his career against John) in the second game of an August 29, 1987, doubleheader. During that four-game series, the only series Sarge played at Yankee Stadium, he went 3-for-11 with two RBIs.

. . . .

I remember it like it was yesterday. Tommy John was on the mound, and I hadn't seen him in a long time. You always used to pad your average against those kinds of guys. I saw him across the way and said, "Tommy's pitching tonight? Hallelujah." I took him deep in Yankee Stadium. Left field. You never forget something like that. When you're going around the bases, you're reflecting on the greatness and the whole aura about Yankee Stadium. You're thinking about the guys who came before you and did so many great things there. And as much as you think about all of that, it really hits you later on. It's really a special place.

. . . .

Utley swatted five home runs and was eliminated after the first round of the Derby. But his appearance wasn't without controversy.

Like most Derby contestants, Utley agreed to wear a microphone during ESPN's live telecast. During the pre-Derby introductions, the sellout crowd at Yankee Stadium (presumably the Mets fans) booed Utley.

"Boo? [Bleep] you," Utley said while standing alongside Florida's Dan Uggla.

The mic picked up the sound, and almost instantly, the video appeared on YouTube.

Utley, embarrassed by the incident, apologized for his "poor choice of words," and ESPN spokesman Nate Smeltz said the cable network's usual five-second delay was enforced only during the actual Derby, not the introductions.

So, Sarge, would you have agreed to wear a mic?

· · · ·

No, not at all. Nope. No way. I was too serious. I didn't have time to be joking around. But television is so big now that nothing really surprises me in terms of guys being mic'd up or whatever. And, really, it's good because it gives fans some more insight. It really does.

JULY 15, 2008

NEW YORK—Brad Lidge will forever remember his second All-Star Game.

Charged with serving as the National League's closer tonight, Lidge warmed up in the ninth, tenth, eleventh, twelfth, thirteenth, and fourteenth innings but sat down each time after the NL failed to take a lead. He had already chucked nearly 100 pitches before he finally entered in the fifteenth, loaded the bases, and allowed Michael Young's sacrifice fly in the American League's 4–3 win in a four-hour, 50-minute marathon, the longest All-Star Game in history.

But there also was the stirring pregame ceremony, featuring almost 50 Hall of Famers at Yankee Stadium. Lidge said he had "goosebumps."

Sarge has never forgotten his All-Star Game appearance either. He represented the Atlanta Braves on the NL team in 1979 at the Kingdome in Seattle.

. . . .

We ended up winning that ballgame 7–6 because of Dave Parker. Remember that throw to home plate [in the eighth inning]? I remember going 0-for-2. I know that I was trying to really force it and made an impact because of Bill Lucas [the late Braves general manager who unexpectedly died of a cerebral hemorrhage two months earlier] and wanted to do something special to really give him the praise for giving me the opportunity to come to Atlanta. That's something I really appreciated. Plus, he was one of the only black general managers at that particular time.

When you saw that ceremony with the Hall of Fame guys [this year], you think of how difficult it is to get to the place where they're at. Not only is it hard work and God-given talent, it's a sacrifice, too. The guys who have been there have, for the most part, had longevity. Not only that, they dominated their particular era.

Seeing [Willie] McCovey out there, playing and having been around him, nobody does it better. He taught me respect of the game, respect of the team you're playing against, not to show anybody up, and to go about your job in a professional way. That's all he ever had to say. When we go out to San Francisco, I sit right up there in the booth with him. He really likes Chase Utley a lot. He studies a lot of the left-handed hitters to see if they bail on left-handed pitchers because he was a hitter that did not. He mentions Chase Utley and how he likes him as a hitter.

But, to be in an All-Star Game, you never forget that. It's a great feeling. You're standing up there knowing, when you look around the room, that all the best players in the league are there. That's a special feeling for any player.

JULY 18, 2008

MIAMI GARDENS—Adam Eaton had his head in the clouds when the Phillies traded for his replacement.

Sitting on the team charter during last night's flight to Miami to resume the season after the All-Star break, Eaton learned the Phillies had swapped three minor leaguers, including second-base prospect Adrian Cardenas, to the Oakland Athletics for right-hander Joe Blanton.

Today, Eaton found out Blanton would take his spot in the rotation.

It wasn't a surprise. Eaton, who signed a three-year, $24.5 million contract before the 2007 season, lugged a 3–8 record and 5.71 ERA to the bullpen for his new role as a long reliever. But he also allowed 14 earned runs in 6⅓ innings over his last two starts, and in his last 13 starts, he has a 6.20 ERA.

Blanton, meanwhile, went 5–12 with a 4.96 ERA for the Athletics. But he is regarded as an "innings-eater," and with CC Sabathia, the pitcher they desired most, having been dealt to the Milwaukee Brewers for a package of prospects that included blue-chip outfielder Matt LaPorta, the Phillies viewed Blanton as a dependable, if unspectacular, consolation prize.

"Anything to help the team," Eaton said before the Phillies (53–46) dropped two of three games to the upstart Marlins and lapsed into a first-place tie with the Mets. "I'd like to be a starter, don't get me wrong. That's not up to me. But I'm on one of the best teams in the big leagues. We're going to win this thing. Whenever they want to give me the ball in whichever situation, I'll be ready."

.   .   .   .

Eaton's a good guy. I thought it was a good move to sign him. But the fact is, early on, looking at Adam Eaton throughout his career, he's been a fly-ball pitcher. I, for one, think that unless you consistently can pitch inside, you can't be a fly-ball pitcher in this particular ballpark [home run–friendly Citizens Bank Park]. However, in saying that, he threw some of his better games against the Mets in New York. The way the Phillies are thinking, it is in there. We just need to get it out more consistently.

It just wasn't to be, for whatever reason. Maybe it was being a little nervous to live up to that contract. Maybe it was just not having the guts to be able to go out there consistently. It's hard to tell. But I've always thought that guys who are in survival modes, who are fighting for their jobs, play harder day in and day out. And Adam, he's definitely not in survival mode.

JULY 22, 2008

NEW YORK—The newest Phillies pitcher is a steak- and chicken-eating country boy who grew up in rural Kentucky, resides in Tennessee, and describes himself as "a low-key guy who would rather fly under the radar." But, really, Joe Blanton would rather not talk at all.

"We used to always walk in the locker room and go, 'Shut up, Joe,' because he'd never say anything," said Florida Marlins catcher John Baker, Blanton's minor league teammate.

Blanton had no prayer of going unnoticed tonight, though. Making his Phillies debut against the Mets in the series-opener at Shea Stadium, with the teams tied atop the NL East and opposed by two-time Cy Young Award–winner Johan Santana, Blanton allowed five runs on eight hits, including a pair of two-run homers by Carlos Delgado and Ramon Castro. By the time he left the game after the sixth inning, the Phils trailed 5–1.

But, in a comeback reminiscent of last September, the Phillies (54–46) scored six runs in the ninth inning and emerged with an 8–6 win that restored their one-game lead in the division and bailed out Blanton.

. . . .

Blanton's an upgrade because the guy pitches inside. And so far, he is throwing more strikes [than Adam Eaton]. You can tell with a pitcher or any player about his demeanor when the camera gets on his face as to whether or not the guy is afraid. Blanton might get hit, but he doesn't seem to be afraid. Talking to him about the pitch Delgado hit out, it was where he wanted it. But, believe it or not, [the Mets] are giving signs from third base, and Delgado was able to see the signs. That's why it's important for the catcher to block the signs. Carlos Delgado is notorious for killing pitchers when he knows what's coming. That ball that he hit out was almost on the ground. The catcher had his glove turned the other way, and he knocked the [stuffing] out of the ball going out of the ballpark.

Pitcher Joe Blanton was acquired from Oakland on July 18 to bolster the starting staff.

People are saying that we shouldn't have given up prospects for Blanton. Well, potential gets managers fired. Period. I want a guy that can do it, that has been proven. When you see rookie players go to the New York Yankees, you known damn well they can probably play, and they play pretty good. Otherwise, they wouldn't be there. You look around the league. [Ryan] Braun, [Troy] Tulowitzki, these guys are playing at a young age and making their own statement. They're adding to the mix. But how many of those guys really are out there? How many of those guys are in our organization? It doesn't take a genius to figure out that we don't have some of those good arms that we see throwing against us. We don't have some of those young players.

JULY 24, 2008

NEW YORK—If, as Hall of Fame manager Earl Weaver once observed, momentum lasts only as long as the next day's starting pitcher, Brett Myers assured the Phillies wouldn't enjoy a lingering carryover from Tuesday night's stirring ninth inning. Making his return last night from his three-week mission to the minors, he walked four batters in a two-run first inning and lasted only five innings in a 6–3 loss to the Mets that reestablished a first-place tie.

But one start isn't enough to determine if Myers is a lost cause.

Far more disconcerting was Jimmy Rollins's behavior in today's series finale.

Nearly an hour before the 12:10 PM matinee against the Mets—and an hour later than the arrival time mandated by Charlie Manuel—Rollins strolled into the clubhouse. He said he opted to drive his car to Shea Stadium rather than take the team bus and explained to Manuel that he had gotten stuck in New York City traffic.

Again, Manuel has two rules: hustle and be on time. Rollins broke the latter, so Manuel erased his name from the lineup.

For the second time in seven weeks, Manuel has disciplined Rollins. On June 5, he benched the National League MVP for not running out a pop fly that was dropped by backpedaling Reds shortstop Paul Janish. In that situation, Rollins agreed with Manuel's decision. This time, he did not, and he expressed little regret for his transgression, reasoning that fill-in Eric Bruntlett got three hits.

Still, the Phillies lost 3–1 and fell out of first place for the first time since May 31.

"We're not going to agree on this one," Rollins said. "I agreed with him last time, but we're not going to agree on this one. I think he understood that, and I understood it. But he's the manager. He has to set a precedent, and for certain players, you are held up to higher rules. That's fine. That's part of it."

. . . .

That's exactly right. As a catalyst of the team, in that situation, you cannot be late when you're fighting for what we're fighting for. There are no excuses. Period. Whether or not he left late, whether or not he got lost, that's immaterial. It shouldn't even be brought up. If you're supposed to be there at a certain time, you have to be there. It means too much to the team. The fact is, you have to be there. For me, you just don't want to be late. This is a game that you've got to make sure you're always on time. It's always better to be an hour early than an hour late. It's simple.

I don't think any less of J-Roll at all. He's a hell of a talent. But he really does have to realize that he has a lot to do with the success and the winning of this ballclub. During the course of the year, we'll talk about different things. On that situation against the Reds, it was something I didn't need to ask about because he handled it the way he did. To bring it up with him, I thought, was beating a dead horse. I want to get around to asking him about this situation here in New York. Really, the only situation was that he was late. It doesn't matter if it was traffic. It doesn't matter if you had a flat tire. If he called and everything and said he was going to be late, then it's a different story. But if he walked in and said, "Hey, there was traffic," then he's wrong. The key is respect of the manager and your teammates. For me, that's where that comes in. Everyone is saying, "Hey, where's J-Roll?" Or they're concerned—did something happen to him? For the guys who really care about him, that would go through their heads.

JULY 27, 2008

PHILADELPHIA—If it was a Sunday home game, it must have involved rain.

The Phillies' run of rain-delayed Sunday matinees at Citizens Bank Park continued today, as they waited out a nearly two-hour thunderstorm before battering the Atlanta Braves' bullpen for a second consecutive comeback victory. In winning the series finale 12–2, the Phils (56–49) took two of three games and stayed one game behind the Mets in the NL East. They also scored 18 runs in 11⅓ innings against the Braves' relievers.

But the day belonged to a far more accomplished reliever, Rich "Goose" Gossage, who was inducted into the Hall of Fame in Cooperstown, New York. Gossage was among the first dominant closers, a snarling flame-thrower with a menacing stare that left hitters quaking. Just ask Sarge, thankful for having to face Gossage only five times and proud of his one hit against him, a solo home run on July 4, 1986.

· · · ·

Going out and having dinner with [Gossage] when he was in Philly [in June], I reminded him of it. He didn't believe I hit a home run. See that's the one thing: I didn't hit a whole lot, and the really good pitchers, I remember them for sure. And one of the reasons I remember Goose so vividly is because the at-bat before that, in the [1984] playoffs, he had struck me out. The next time I see him, I hit a home run, and I'm going around the bases saying, "Two years too late," because it would've been a three-run home run to tie the game in the playoffs. I remember it vividly. He didn't.

He was very intimidating, and I'm glad I didn't face him more. He's the type of pitcher that, you'd be in the outfield and you wouldn't even have to turn and look at him [in the bullpen], you'd hear the sound of the glove popping. Then, instantly, you'd try to remember where you were in the lineup, and gratification would come to you when you made the last out because you knew you wouldn't be going up and facing him. He had a scowl on his face. He was a hard thrower. He was effectively wild, if you will, and he used that. He was an intimidator. And he'd go two or three innings for saves. We wouldn't dare do that with [Brad] Lidge, unless maybe it was the World Series or something. That's why he's a Hall of Famer.

JULY 29, 2008

WASHINGTON—When the tying run reached first base in the eighth inning tonight, Charlie Manuel lumbered to the mound to take the ball from Brett Myers.

"Check my numbers against this guy," Myers hollered.

Speechless, Manuel recoiled.

Myers busted out laughing.

It has been a while since he had so much fun on a major league mound, even longer since he won a major league game. Myers did both in the nation's capital. He allowed only an unearned run in the eighth inning and flummoxed the feeble-hitting Nationals in a 2–1 victory, Myers's first since May 30 and first on the road all season. The Phillies (57–49) remained a half-game behind in the division.

· · · ·

The jury's still out on Brett. It was good to see him do what he did. That's certainly more encouraging than what we have seen. But, for me, those guys in Texas can hit. There aren't as many good hitters in Washington. I want to see that kind of swagger when we're playing against the Mets, when we're playing against Florida, when we're playing against L.A. I want to see that swagger when you're coming off in the seventh inning, and it's a job well-done.

JULY 31, 2008

WASHINGTON—About 10 days ago, Shane Victorino asked a few Phillies beat writers if they had heard any juicy trade rumors. One, in fact, involved Victorino going to the Colorado Rockies in a multiplayer blockbuster for Matt Holliday. Since then, Victorino has admitted to Googling his name to monitor trade innuendo, and before batting practice yesterday, he walked through the Phillies' clubhouse in Washington and said, "Twenty-three more hours to go."

Clearly, he's preoccupied by the trade deadline.

But the 4:00 PM time limit came and went today with the Phillies not making any moves. It wasn't for a lack of trying. General manager Pat Gillick said they were nearing a three-team trade that would've landed a mid-level starting pitcher, and he admitted they had discussions (and reservations) about acquiring Manny Ramirez. The Phillies' biggest need, a left-handed reliever, went unaddressed because teams were seeking elite prospects for the likes of Ron Mahay, Jack Taschner, and John Grabow.

So, with their roster intact, the Phillies (59–49) completed a sweep of the Nationals and moved one game ahead of the Mets.

.   .   .   .

I think [the trade deadline] can work two ways. I think it can be a distraction, for sure. I think it can also be a motivation. With this team, where it's a little more close-knit like a family, I think that makes it difficult because you get comfortable and you don't want to move. If you're going to another team, and they're not winning, it's just an awful letdown. It's a nervous time. First of all, the player can't do anything about it, unless you have a no-trade [clause]. But even with players that have a no-trade, if you're not wanted there, you've got to go. A lot of times, players don't understand that. Once it gets to where it's personal, it makes it even worse. But I made it a point personally that every time I saw that club, I kind of reminded them of the wrong decision that they made.

With Victorino, all of a sudden, with him shortening his swing and making solid contact, it makes it where he's almost an untouchable. I mean, look at what he's bringing to the table. Defense. Speed. And that first and second hitter that they have, with J-Roll and Victorino, it's working out the way they want. If the right is not working, well, the left is. Victorino certainly has been getting on base over the past two or three weeks. He has been coming up with some big home runs. Holliday is an MVP-type player, but with the makeup of our club, it would've been a disaster because nobody would've been able to play center except for maybe [Jayson] Werth. I guess they would've put him there. But, still, they invested in [Geoff] Jenkins, so what are they going to do with him? Then, he gets no playing time. They probably would like that situation, even with the defense that Holliday doesn't play, if maybe they had him instead of Pat [Burrell] and then still be able to have Victorino. But if you've got Pat and Holliday in the outfield, you're going to kill Werth. Then, besides, you end up getting more power but less speed. There are times defensively when Victorino has won the game with his arm or running out a fly ball.

I, for one, am glad they didn't make that deal. To be quite frank, if they were hitting the way they should, we wouldn't be talking about getting an extra player. These guys should be hitting better. J-Roll should be. The league is set up for guys to hit 35 [home runs] and 100 [RBIs]. You hit a certain amount of home runs, it's pretty difficult not to get paid.

I was dealt one time at the deadline. Well, it was a few weeks earlier going to Seattle [in 1987], which was really unfortunate because I had the opportunity to go to Minnesota. They won it all that year, and I was in Seattle, which was a long way away. That was bad luck. Dallas Green called me in, in spring training and said not to get angry, that they're not going to be playing me, they're going to try and deal me, so try and bear with it. I would've loved to play with Andre Dawson, but I was traded to Seattle. That was a good experience, though.

Chapter 7

AUGUST

AUGUST 1, 2008

ST. LOUIS—As he walked into Busch Stadium, Jimmy Rollins pondered better days.

Seven weeks ago, on Friday the 13th of June, the Phillies opened a three-game series in St. Louis by thumping the Cardinals 20–2. According to the Elias Sports Bureau, a Phillies team hadn't scored 20 runs in a game twice in one season since 1900. But this 2008 Murderer's Row rang up a 20-spot twice in 19 days and was averaging 5.41 runs per game.

Since then, though, the Phillies are batting .248. They have scored 173 runs, an average of 4.44 per game, and they have gone 18–21 during a stretch in which their lead in the National League East has been sliced from four games over the surprising Florida Marlins to one game over the revived New York Mets.

So, upon returning to St. Louis, Rollins grasped for some good karma.

"I've thought about that, honestly," he said. "This is where it started to go bad. But we're playing good now, so hopefully, this is where it starts to go great."

Well, so much for that. Old friend Kyle Lohse held his former teammates to three runs on five hits in 5⅔ innings before three relievers kept the Phillies (59–50) hitless in the Cardinals' 6–3 victory over ace lefty Cole Hamels.

· · · ·

I'm not down there every day, but one of the problems that I see from upstairs is it seems that the guys are guessing a little bit too much and guessing wrong. In situations where you want to be able to try and pull the ball, they might swing early in the count and not allow themselves a pitch to be able to execute. That has to do with more mental strength. You've got to be mentally strong in a situation. Guy on second, I've got to get him over. If my best way is to hit the ball on the right side, good. If my best way is to hit a long fly ball, good. You've got to be able to bunt. I think the situation enters the guys' minds, but their strokes tell me that they're not in the best position to hit the ball the other way. They might be out in front, which means you're going to pull the ball. You've got to be strong mentally. You've got to want an advantage. Every player, pitching-wise or hitting-wise, has got to have an advantage.

I thought Milton Bradley would've fit on this team like a glove. But he doesn't fit the mold. He's too much of a kick-ass, which they need. [Aaron] Rowand was that way, but it was more opposite. It was by his play, going through walls or giving his body, no matter what. People say none of the guys are having a career year. But look at us in '83. Nobody had an MVP year. The same with this club. Nobody is having an MVP year, really, except for [closer Brad] Lidge. But you could still win it even without that.

You would think that they have a run in them when everyone gets hot. We have a tendency to take it for granted—when they're hitting the way they that they hit—that they can come back on a particular pitcher. You'll be able to tell when they're doing that because it'll show. They have too many good professional hitters to go this long without being able to hit the ball. I think you couldn't say that if they've never done it. But because they have, you're always looking for them to get back to where they were. It isn't like they can't do it. It's just that they haven't done it. So you never give up, ever, because you never know how the season is going to go. It might boil down to the last game, and they need to win it with hits, and now, all of a sudden, that's when they start. Maybe that propels you right there.

AUGUST 6, 2008

PHILADELPHIA—Wherever he went last winter—from team promotional banquets in Philadelphia and Allentown, Pennsylvania, to speaking engagements near his home in Winter Haven, Florida—Charlie Manuel referred to 40-year-old reliever Tom "Flash" Gordon as the linchpin of the Phillies' bullpen.

Thus, tonight's announcement in the press box sounded grim.

Gordon, sidelined since July 5 by right elbow inflammation, walked off the mound in the first inning of a start for Class A Clearwater complaining of elbow pain. The Phillies were hoping he would be ready to return to the bullpen by next week. Instead, Gordon will fly to Philadelphia to meet with team physician

Dr. Michael Ciccotti. If surgery is necessary—and even the most optimistic team officials are not ruling it out—Ciccotti's diagnosis will be the death knell to Gordon's season and perhaps his 20-year career.

Since he broke into the majors with the Kansas City Royals in 1988, Gordon has been a starter, a closer, and a setup reliever. He won 17 games and finished second in the American League Rookie of the Year voting in 1989, led the league with 46 saves in 1998, set a then–major league record with 54 consecutive saves from 1998 to 1999, pitched in three All-Star Games, and overcame elbow ligament replacement surgery in 1999.

Gordon posted a 1.32 ERA in his final 15 appearances last season, and after yielding five runs in the ninth inning Opening Day, he went 5–1 with a 2.13 ERA over his next 27 outings, proving he could be consistently effective. With 138 career wins and 158 saves, he's part of pitching's exclusive 15-member 100–100 club, joining Hoyt Wilhelm, Rollie Fingers, Dennis Eckersley, Goose Gossage, Dave Giusti, Bob Stanley, Ron Reed, John Smoltz, Lindy McDaniel, Ron Kine, Roy Face, Stu Miller, Ellis Kinder, and Firpo Marberry.

After the season, the Phillies must decide whether to pick up their $4.5 million option on Gordon's contract for 2009. For now, though, they will rely on Ryan Madson and converted starter Chad Durbin as the primary right-handers in the seventh and eighth innings. And although Manuel is concerned about overusing them down the stretch, they combined for three scoreless innings in relief of Kyle Kendrick in tonight's 5–0 win over the Florida Marlins that moved the Phillies (62–51) to 2½ games ahead of the Mets.

· · · ·

Flash is one of my favorite guys. Quite a warrior. In his day, nobody did it better. You don't like to see guys get beat up when they don't have their good stuff, but he proved last

September and for most of this year, that he still has good stuff. The main thing is health. He's done very well in this game. Nobody wants to leave on an injury, but if you're not able to pitch the way that you normally would, then there's nothing else you can do. It happens to everybody. Your ability just doesn't allow you to do it. To be held out there and know that a guy is hitting you like he shouldn't be hitting you, that doesn't make you feel good. Curt Schilling is going through the same thing right now. If he comes back and doesn't have his good stuff, he's not going to come back out here and get beat around. With Flash, if he's able to come back pain-free, he'll be fine. He'll be able to pitch. There's room for that kind of arm here. Anyone who's throwing 90 with a breaking ball, that's impressive. His breaking ball wasn't as sharp as it was before. That's all. But that might have something to do with how he's feeling.

That said, it's a huge loss. However, Chad Durbin has proven he can step in there. From the left side, J.C. Romero has proven he's got ice in his veins. So, I still think, with their pitching, they can get there. Pitching has not been a problem, even with Flash not here. It's been strictly offense, not putting together enough hits and, again, not hitting enough balls hard. That's the biggest thing right now, even bigger than losing Flash.

AUGUST 7, 2008

PHILADELPHIA—The diagnosis is predictably ominous.

After today's 3–0 loss in the series finale against the Florida Marlins, the Phillies (62–52) learned that Tom Gordon, their 40-year-old setup reliever, has sustained damage to the ulnar collateral ligament in his right elbow and may require surgery. And although Gordon will seek a second opinion in Los Angeles from orthopedic surgeon Dr. Lewis Yocum, it's almost certain that the Phillies will have to subtract him from their bullpen plans.

So they have added Scott Eyre.

Two days ago, the Chicago Cubs designated Eyre for assignment, and the Phillies acquired him today for Class A right-hander Brian Schlitter. Eyre, 36, fell out of favor in Chicago after a pair of injuries (left elbow inflammation and a groin strain) landed him on the disabled list. But he didn't allow a run in his first 14 appearances, and he figures to give the Phillies another lefty reliever to pair with J.C. Romero.

The Phillies tried to sign Eyre before the 2006 season, even dispatching pitching coach Rich Dubee to take him on a recruiting lunch. Eyre opted for a three-year, $11 million contract from the Cubs, and when he walked into the Phillies' clubhouse, Dubee greeted him by saying, "Two years late."

Better late than never, though.

. . . .

I think it's great. First of all, the guy hasn't been overused, because he was hurt. He's coming over here with, what, 12⅓ innings? So, you know he has some stuff left. Then, surprisingly, he's been throwing 92. He's a veteran pitcher, and he's not afraid. Those are the guys you can use if they're not used up. With the way that Charlie [Manuel] has been using the left-handers, this is great because maybe in that fifth, when you need to get a tough lefty out, you don't have to use [Clay] Condrey or [Ryan] Madson. You can use that lefty, and now, you're not burning up J.C. for the latter part of the game.

The Cubs didn't want him. They have an abundance of talent now with all the acquisitions. To me, that's what the good general managers always do. They know who's overloaded now with pitching. There's going to be decisions some teams have to make. That's how we ended up getting J.C. last year from Boston. Same thing. And look how that worked out for us.

AUGUST 8, 2008

PHILADELPHIA—Two years ago, when the Phillies overhauled Charlie Manuel's coaching staff after falling short of a playoff berth, the short list of third-base-coach candidates included Juan Samuel.

It didn't work out.

Samuel, the popular former Phillies second baseman, had skippered the New York Mets' Double A club in Binghamton, New York, in 2006. He wanted to return to the majors, but he also wanted a multiyear contract. With Manuel heading into the last year of his deal, the Phillies weren't willing to give new coaches more than a one-year guarantee, leaving Samuel to sign a his multiyear deal to be the Orioles' third-base and infield coach.

The Phillies haven't forgotten him, though.

Before the offense fell deadly silent in a 2–0, 12-inning loss to the Pittsburgh Pirates, the Phils inducted Samuel into the Wall of Fame at Citizens Bank Park, the first event in a three-day Alumni Weekend that will reunite nearly 50 former Phillies players. Samuel, 47, made his major league debut on August 24, 1983, and batted .277 in 18 games to help the Phillies' charge for the National League East crown.

Ten members of the 1983 team, including Sarge and Sammy, participated in Alumni Weekend festivities. They were joined by Hall of Famers Mike Schmidt and

Steve Carlton, pitchers Al Holland, Larry Andersen, and Marty Bystrom, catcher Ozzie Virgil, outfielder Garry Maddox, and coach Bobby Wine.

.   .   .   .

It's always great, always a good time. You don't get to see these guys a lot. Steve Carlton, Mike Schmidt. I get to play golf with him in spring training. Samuel, you think of the attitude that he still exemplifies, like he did when he was playing. Really, one of these days, I expect for him to be a coach here. He's such a fan favorite for me. We'll see what happens with that. Sammy had talent and speed. But no one knows, honestly, until you see a guy a couple years if he's going to last. Even the stars you have, you never know how they're going to play. When [Chase] Utley first came and [Placido] Polanco was there at second base, you never thought Utley would be doing what he's doing right now. Quite frankly, there were a lot of people saying he wasn't going to really make it. I guess he fooled them.

I had a good time every single place I played. For me, getting to the World Series here [in 1983] was major. But getting to the postseason in '84, where the Cubs hadn't been for a long time, it was really major coming one game away from absolutely being heroes. And when you grow up in the San Francisco Giants organization, how can you not like that? Being involved with [Willie] Mays and [Willie] McCovey, and then, winning Rookie of the Year there. I really had a great, special time every place that I've gone. When you're a rookie, you don't care where you're playing. But once you start playing, and you come to a team like the Phillies, you realize how great it is to be with players who can really play. All of a sudden, you're not the main guy, and it's really gratifying. Then, to go to the Cubs and have a lot to do with their success, it's very gratifying. I liked them all. They really are special. Growing up and being Willie McCovey's locker partner, it doesn't get better than that. To talk with him to this day, or Hank Aaron, or Maury Wills, that's special kind of stuff.

But the Phillies do as good a job as any team as far as having fans remember players that have played here before. They have a deep tradition, for sure. I think that's why you have so many players that, even from Robin Roberts's era, are still involved in coming back because of the treatment they get from the Phillies after all these years. There's a sincere tribute, right there.

AUGUST 9, 2008

PHILADELPHIA—Eleven nights ago, upon being removed in the eighth inning of a game at Washington, Brett Myers feigned anger by yelling at Charlie Manuel.

This time, he wasn't pretending.

Myers, making his fourth start since returning from his convalescence to the minors, was one out from completing the eighth inning tonight against the Pittsburgh Pirates when Manuel lumbered to the mound and replaced him after only 93 pitches. Myers hollered in frustration, handed the ball to Manuel without making eye contact, then gave an exaggerated wave of his cap to an appreciative sell-out crowd at Citizens Bank Park.

When Big Chuck returned to the dugout, he confronted Myers, the one-time amateur boxer who continued walking before turning and coming nose-to-nose

Charlie Manuel and Brett Myers exchanged words in the dugout after the pitcher was pulled on August 9 against the Pirates.

with his manager in a heated exchange. They laughed about it later, easy to do after the Phillies (63–53) beat the lowly Pirates 4–2 to maintain their hold on first place. Manuel called it "just two strong-willed people who disagreed." And although it appeared to be a potentially volatile situation, it was another sign that Myers, always emotional, has regained his confidence.

"I'm a competitor," said Myers, 2–0 with a 2.10 ERA in four starts since his return. "I let my emotions get the best of me sometimes. You've got to control your emotions, and I didn't do a good job of that. But we're all patched up. We're still buddies."

.   .   .   .

Yeah, Myers was a little hot. He showed some emotion. It wasn't right what he did. He has to be careful because I know managers that, when things get tough, they might leave you out there a little while, see if you can't work your own self out. Charlie's a good man and takes a lot of heat for not just Brett but a lot of his players, and he expects the same thing. One of the statements I got from reading Myers's face was, "This is my ballgame." Well, no, it's not. It's our ballgame. It's not an individual game. But I think that he learned something after that ballgame.

It's the heat of the moment. People have to realize that there are certain times that people are going to react in a way that, if it's a normal situation, they wouldn't. This is 162 ballgames. You get frustrated. You want to win. You feel good out there on the mound, and all of a sudden, pitch counts don't really mean anything. But the bottom line is—and I think this is one of the greatest statements of all time—Ryne Sandberg gave a speech at the Hall of Fame and said, "When does the name on the back of the uniform become more important than the name on the front?" In other words, when does "Sandberg" become more important than the "Cubs"? That tells the story. You win as the Chicago Cubs, not as Ryne Sandberg. It's a sacrifice to be able to win. You have to sacrifice stats with that. I mean, Mike [Schmidt] could've had individual records his entire life.

One thing about Brett: he has been pitching better. We'll see how he does against some of the better teams. He'll have L.A. in his next start. We'll see what happens. It looks like he's kind of back. He's relying on his fastball again instead of the cutter. It's all about results. He's not throwing any harder. He is hitting some spots. The fact is, when you get results, and when you start going into the seventh inning with the score the way it is, and he knows that he's pitched a hell of a ballgame, and they put the camera on his face, you can see that he means business. It looks like he has that swagger that he normally has, which is good to see.

AUGUST 10, 2008

PHILADELPHIA—For a second straight game, the situation called for the Phillies' All-Star closer to pitch the ninth inning.

But, for a second straight game, Brad Lidge was unavailable.

Lidge revealed today that he has been diagnosed with mild shoulder tendinitis and has been taking anti-inflammatory medication to quell the "sluggish" feeling in his right arm. Neither Lidge nor Charlie Manuel are overly concerned that the problem will linger, but it is considered serious enough to shut him down for a few days.

The Mets also have concerns about their closer. Billy Wagner went on the disabled list last week with a strained left forearm, and it is not known when he'll be able to pitch again. Manuel suggested that Lidge's woes may have started when he warmed up six times—and tossed more than 100 pitches—before finally pitching the fifteenth inning of the All-Star Game on July 15 at Yankee Stadium. But Lidge believes the shoulder stiffness stems from a glitch in his mechanics that was discovered last week by pitching coach Rich Dubee.

Regardless, few of Lidge's recent outings have gone smoothly. He's 28-for-28 in save opportunities, including 8-for-8 since the All-Star Game. But he has walked seven batters in his last 7⅓ innings and put runners on base in eight of his last 11 appearances. Of his last 209 pitches, only 122 have been strikes.

"Taking a day or two here will pay off big for me," Lidge said before the Phillies (64–53) closed out a 6–3 victory over the Pittsburgh Pirates in which Greg Dobbs set a single-season mark with his 21st pinch-hit. "I'm not real worried about anything, but at the same time, you want to make sure you're not just plowing through something and making it worse."

. . . .

Every club has to have a closer. If you don't have that, it's going to be difficult to win. Look at New York with Wagner. With the way they're playing, to be saying, "Okay, we don't have our closer," that experience goes a long, long way. Even if you have someone who throws just as hard, not having the guy with that experience puts another wrinkle in the National League East. So you just hope that a few days off will get Lidge going again.

But again, from our side of it, you would feel better with that statement if the guys were hitting like they're capable of hitting. My concern is they're not consistently hitting the ball hard. If you're not doing that, it shows that you're going to be in that slump longer. The home run is a given. I want to see some shots up the gap or some line drives up the middle or some hard-hit ground balls. Since the All-Star break, it hasn't been as consistent as the team would like, to where you really feel comfortable. Like last year, even though they were behind, you felt comfortable in saying, "These guys are going to win" because of the swagger that they had going on the field on a daily basis. There was no lead that was safe for any team. I don't know if they feel that way right now. I don't know if they feel like, "Okay, I'm getting ready to knock the [stuffing] out of the ball."

Right now, on this particular date, I don't see the eye of the tiger. I see them going out and not wanting to lose, instead of going out and feeling confident that they're going to win. But I don't see them going out and doing everything they can to stop them from losing. Like I said on the road, the guys are doing a lot of first-pitch swinging. They struck out more than 60 times on the road. If you look at us in '83, compared to what they're doing right now, we probably were just as dismal. We had no one that really excelled. The only thing was we came together in September. I remember Joe Morgan saying if we were close, he'd make sure we were there. And, by God, we were close and we went to town in September. We won a [ton] of ballgames to get us into post-season. They might have just as good or better talent on this team, but mentally, they're nowhere near as strong. Nowhere near.

AUGUST 14, 2008

LOS ANGELES—Gigi Rollins has always told her oldest son to speak his mind.

And Jimmy Rollins listens to his mother.

"When I'm asked a question," he said, "I don't try to be politically correct. If I feel a certain way, that's pretty much what you're going to get. I probably get that from my mother more than anything. She always says, 'Baby, if you're going to talk the talk, you have to walk the walk. If you're going to say something, you deliver. If you don't, be prepared to get crushed.' "

Last season, Rollins raised his profile with his shoot-from-the-lip style. After his off-season boast that the Phillies would be the "team to beat" in the NL East, he became the first player in history with at least 200 hits, 20 triples, 30 homers, and 30 steals in a season; led the Phillies to the division title over the Mets; and won the NL MVP Award.

Sometimes, though, his candid answers get him in trouble.

Yesterday, before heading to Dodger Stadium, Rollins and Ryan Howard were studio guests on Fox Sports's *Best Damn Sports Show Period*. Asked if Philly is as tough as its reputation for being a demanding sports town, Rollins said, "It can be, yeah. There are times, like, it's one of those cities. I might catch some flak for saying this, but, you know, they're front-runners. When you're doing good, they're on your side. When you're doing bad, they're completely against you."

After the show aired, the phone lines at Philadelphia's sports radio stations were lit up by calls from offended fans. And today, Rollins, benched earlier this season for not hustling and showing up late for a game in New York, phoned *Best Damn Sports Show Period* to clarify, but not to retract, his comments. He admitted he misused the term "front-runners," but called for fans to give off less "negative energy" and to offer unconditional positive reinforcement, whether the Phillies are winning or losing.

Meanwhile, the Phillies (64–57) haven't won at all on the West Coast. After falling 8–6 and 4–3 in the first two games against the Dodgers, they turned a 6–1 lead into a crushing 7–6 loss Wednesday night before dropping the series finale 3–1 today and falling into second place, one game behind the New York Mets.

. . . .

I think what he said is true. Absolutely. And to take it further, not only is it a tough place to play in all the sports, they expect excellence on a daily basis. When they don't get it, they show you in the way of boos. The seed already was planted, so he just put water on it. They booed me for the first two or three weeks [in 1981] when we got off to a slow start. Keep in mind, they booed me just because I was in left field, taking Greg Luzinski's place. And it wasn't even like I was traded for him. I felt, eventually, that they would warm up to me, and it happened. You get your respect by doing, not by saying. It's a no-nonsense city in terms of their sports and in terms of their athletes going out and excelling. That's what makes the place so special. Not everybody can play in this type of circumstance. Some people get nervous with the stands filled the way they are and fans of today coming out and showing their displeasure in boos. We would get displeasure in bottles and stuff like that. In my era, we used it mostly as motivation. Go boo Pete Rose and see how many hits he gets. Tony Perez, Garry Maddox, Mike Schmidt. Who got booed more than Mike? When we were on the road, if Mike was having a bad road trip, there was this one guy on the right-field side at home. Mike'd say, "This guy is getting ready to boo me, and I can hear his voice louder than I can anyone out there." Mike would hear it. The thing that Jimmy is talking about is hearing it at home. They're about the same in Chicago. It used to be different, but now, you have a new generation. This is what a lot of the players should understand. They show their displeasure in that way, period, at all the ballparks, for the most part. They may not boo you in San Diego. But the White Sox, Cubs, Yankees, Boston, Philly, they boo. Not everyone can play under those circumstances. But when you have a ballpark filled and you're a game and a half out, that gives [the fans] incentive enough to take you on, even if you're a little tired.

There are different ways to look at what he said. But when fans think, "Well, you're calling us front-runners," they came out and said with their complaints, "We'll show you." I think any time the ballpark is filled the way that it has been, or even if it isn't, once you get between the lines, that's why they call it The Show. You've got to put on a show. That's by always hustling, and giving your ultimate at the plate or on the mound. You end up judging your true talent on your team. When your hitters are able to hit in the seventh, eighth, and ninth innings, and when the pitching is able to get guys out in the seventh, eighth, and ninth innings, you can judge players that way. Last year, clutch hit after clutch hit, J-Roll was coming up with them. He had a tremendous year, and obviously, that was why he was the MVP.

But this game is very humbling. You can be on top of the world one day and down here the next day, where nobody even knows your name. It goes by so quick, too. A lot of time, players don't realize it. When you're playing, people will do anything for you, almost too much. You get invited to everything. But when you're out of the club, you're out of the club. You're always from the outside looking in. Even guys who have actually played, players can be distant because of being burned before. Now, one thing, and I don't know if J-Roll realizes it, is everybody doesn't win MVPs every year. But for this team to win it and for him not to have a good year, he would be an MVP back in Philly anyway. Because things aren't going well for him. I don't know if he's thinking, "Oh, well, I'm not going to be able to reach my goals." He's giving the effort, but he doesn't have the fire with the effort. Keep in mind, last year, not only [Ryan] Howard went down, [Chase] Utley went down. And J-Roll carried the ballclub. So it's not like he can't do it. It goes to show you what one guy really meant to his particular ballclub. That's not to say, if he's not on this club that the Philadelphia Phillies won't have a product to put out on the field. The show is going to continue, no matter who leaves the game. Players today are a little bit more sensitive, to say the least, and only want to see their name in bold print when things are going good. I don't think J-Roll is that kind of player. What Jimmy did is take the heat off of the players and put it on himself. He said yesterday, "Don't boo my teammates. Boo me." For me, I can be in a foxhole any day with a guy like that.

AUGUST 19, 2008

SAN DIEGO—Jamie Moyer and Greg Maddux refuse to act their age.

Two nights ago, in the opener of a three-game series at Petco Park, the Phillies outlasted the Padres 1–0 with their respective 40-something pitchers on the mound. Moyer—at 45, the majors' oldest player—allowed three hits and threw only 98 pitches in seven scoreless innings. Meanwhile, Maddux, 42, gave up little more than a solo homer to Pat Burrell and threw 85 pitches in seven innings.

"It just goes to show that, when you know what you're doing with the baseball, you don't have to throw 95 to 100 to get it done," Charlie Manuel said. "That's what it shows. Good command is what it's all about. Putting the ball where you want it."

Lately, Kyle Kendrick hasn't had very good command.

Last night, the weak-hitting Padres pummeled Kendrick for six runs in only 3⅔ innings, marking his second straight wretched start. So, before the Phillies (66–58) notched a 4–3 win tonight and wrapped the West Coast swing with a 2–5 record, Moyer set up a 40-minute chat between Kendrick and Maddux in the outfield during batting practice.

"I don't know what it is," Kendrick said. "It's like I'm afraid of contact or something."

Said Maddux, a 353-game winner, "I'm afraid of contact, too. Nobody wants to get hit."

Right then, Kendrick felt better.

"He kind of talked to me," said Kendrick, who wasn't even two years old when Moyer and Maddux were rookies on a 1986 Cubs team that featured Sarge in left field. "He's been there. We talked about [developing] the change-up, what he sees in hitters. I was real fortunate to be able to talk to him for so long."

. . . .

I think that anyone should seek out knowledge of older players who have been in the game. If you're a second baseman, I'd seek out information from the best second baseman. If you have a chance to talk to a guy like Ivan Rodriguez, I'd say you owe it to yourself to do that. There are some tricks of the trade that Keith Hernandez can teach a first baseman. Why wouldn't you want to know that? I would. The knowledge is there to be had. Kendrick, he looks scared to death to me. I've seen that look on guys before, and that's where you talk about an advantage. Manny Ramirez and those guys, they're sharks. When they see you like that, they feast on your butt like there's no end. He was done, scared to death, like a deer in headlights. These are the things that young pitchers go through. That's the difference when you look at Greg Maddux and Jamie Moyer. Where Kyle Kendrick is trying to make a great pitch, Jamie and Greg, they're just trying to make a good pitch because they know the hitter is going to get himself out most of the time. Kendrick is falling behind, not getting close to the dish. I would think they have him on a short leash right now, give him one or two more starts. I'm just thinking. I'm just looking at it. They're not going to continue to go through that.

When I see Greg and Jamie, I'm in awe. The velocity isn't there, but mentally, they're very strong. From what I hear, Maddux easily could have another six, seven victories with the way he's pitched. I don't know you could say that for Moyer. But he's certainly done such a heck of a job in getting the most out of his ability. There are people who are saying he doesn't have a choice, that with all the kids he has [Moyer has six children], he has to keep pitching. But the one thing you like about Jamie is that he gives back. Not just in this community, in a lot of communities.

I remember them back in '86. Both of them didn't say a word. They were rookie pitchers. Everyday players didn't really talk to those guys all the time. We had [Rick] Sutcliffe on the team, [Dennis] Eckersley. Those are some guys who had been around the block, and these two guys had just got there. When Daniel Cey, Ron Cey's son, and my son Junior were there, they used to be hanging out in the dugout and so on. Jamie had a chance to pitch against Junior, and he always told me he was going to put one in his ribs because he always hit him so good. I told him, "Go ahead. It would be like hitting your own kid." I said, "Don't tell me about it. Go ahead." I don't know if he's faced him since, but I don't think he ever got around to hitting him in the ribs. He couldn't do that.

AUGUST 22, 2008

PHILADELPHIA—Since returning to Citizens Bank Park three nights ago, Jimmy Rollins has gotten booed by the grudge-holding masses (not surprising), resurgent

Brett Myers tossed his first shutout since May 20, 2004, and his first complete game since September 20, 2006, (somewhat surprising), and the Phillies missed an opportunity to sweep the sad-sack Washington Nationals and slipping 2½ games off the Mets' pace in the NL East (very surprising).

But, at least for one night, Ryan Howard found a cure for his slump.

Watch video.

"I've told him, I want him to go back and look at his 2006 [NL MVP] tape and study it, his swing and his approach, and I want him to get back to that swing," Charlie Manuel said today. "That's what I want because he hit breaking balls and he hit change-ups and he hit fastballs."

Howard, unlike video addict Chase Utley, isn't keen on watching film unless it's a pregame movie. But, as Sarge always told his hitters in Toronto, Chicago, and Milwaukee, studying video can be an instructive tool. Howard listened to Manuel, and sure enough, in the fourth inning tonight, he rekindled memories of 2006 by swatting an opposite-field, two-run home run to fuel an 8–1 laugher in the series-opener against the Los Angeles Dodgers.

"He followed the ball better, and he had real good, smooth swings," Manuel said after Kyle Kendrick outpitched new mentor Greg Maddux, who was traded to the Dodgers earlier this week. "I told him, 'All you've got to do is look at some film.'"

Simple, right?

. . . .

I think video can help for sure because you're able to point out if a guy is coming off the ball. Personally, I never liked to look at negative stuff. I'd go in and check out maybe a ball going out of the ballpark or a long drive up the middle. I want to be positive, and I want to see what I'm doing when things are positive. Now, if it's a long period of time, absolutely. [Willie] Mays always talked about guys going into slumps. Everybody is going to do it, but the hitter that can get out of it the quickest is going to be the best hitter. If you notice, and it happens with every single guy when they're in a slump, when they take that first pitch, it's always right down the middle. Now, he gets ready to swing at some ball that's sinking or whatever, and that's the one you have to swing at. Sometimes you have to get back to being aggressive, and sometimes you have to know when to back off.

Whatever the hitters feel it would take to get them back to where they should be, I was all for that. Too many of the guys today, they think about the final product, as in the hit. You have to think about your position that allows you to do the hitting. That's why I always preach about [Jayson] Werth being back on his heels. But when he's solid and he's going into the ball and not bailing, gosh, he's as good as any of them. In the home-run contest, I'll take Werth and spot you guys. That's how much confidence I have in the way he swings. With Ryan, when he's going well, I don't know if it's being more patient, but he's swinging at more strikes. That's something he can probably see on video, how they're pitching him and what they're trying to do.

AUGUST 25, 2008

PHILADELPHIA—Jimmy Rollins already had driven in two runs, scored a third, tallied more hits through six innings (three) than he had in his previous six games (two), and turned all the boos to cheers.

But there was Brett Myers, facing Manny Ramirez, one pitch from undoing it all.

A month ago, he probably would have. Myers may have uncorked a flat fastball, maybe a cutter, and Manny would have launched it into the stratosphere for a grand slam to erase the Phillies' three-run lead. But this is a different Myers. Since he came back from the minors, his fastball is crisper, his control sharper, and his swagger—always his best trait—has returned.

So, after tossing two fastballs, Myers got Ramirez to line a curveball to right field, where Jayson Werth tracked and caught it. And despite allowing 13 hits and 16 runners, the Phillies won 5–0 tonight and secured their first four-game sweep of the Dodgers since August 29 through September 1, 1985, in Los Angeles and their first ever against them in Philadelphia. The Phils (72–59) moved within a half-game of the Mets, who are bound for Citizens Bank Park tomorrow to open a two-game series.

After his pivotal at-bat in the seventh inning, Ramirez, 2-for-14 without any home runs or RBIs in the series, shouted to Myers as he walked off the field. Myers pointed toward him, an acknowledgment from one competitor to another.

"We've talked before," said Myers, 4–1 with a 1.66 ERA since his stint in the minors. "He's a good dude. He's very honest with how he feels about certain pitchers and stuff like that. It's a good compliment from him that I'm tough to get a hit off of, I guess."

·   ·   ·   ·

What you like, and what I've seen in this homestand against the Dodgers, is that payback is just so gratifying. You know, after they beat us four straight in L.A., I'm telling you, to have my boy Larry [Bowa] coming in chirping and they don't even get one game, that's a good feeling. The guys feel good about that. They got embarrassed in L.A., so they came back and said, "Hey, take a little taste of this pudding." It was like '83. We lost 11 out of 12 to the Dodgers, and then we got in the playoffs and beat them [with Sarge batting .429 with three home runs and eight RBIs to win the NLCS MVP]. That was sweet. You know, the left fielder did okay that series. He did okay.

The Dodgers have a pretty good guy in left field now. Manny's a guy who can hit. He knows that, from 60'6", there ain't a guy alive when he's right that can get him out. They're going to, of course. But his thinking is that he just goes out there with his approach, and that allows him to maximize his ability. The people in Boston, they're not surprised at Manny doing what he's doing. They're pissed off that he's not there doing it. But after a while, they just got fed up, and it was time to move on. If [the Phillies] got Manny Ramirez, who sits on this club? I think Pat [Burrell] would've sat. I don't know if a lot of clubs wanted to get him right now. Pat would've sat. Jayson [Werth] would've played because he was hitting. He was coming. I don't think we had enough to get him, but whoever they had to deal, the outfielders that are here now were still going to be here, I think. And one of them was going to have to sit because Manny was going to have to play every day. Manny made his point, though, and I know one thing, he's another guy who, if you can harness and get him right, he can make your club so much better because he's a professional hitter.

AUGUST 26–27, 2008

PHILADELPHIA—Once it was finally over, and the Phillies had turned a seven-run deficit into an interminable, improbable 8–7 victory in a 13-inning, 5-hour and 17-minute marathon, Jimmy Rollins stood at his locker at 2:00 in the morning and explained where they found the fortitude for another crazy comeback against the rival New York Mets.

"The other team gives you some inspiration, let's put it that way," Rollins said after going 5-for-7 and coming one hit short of matching Jayson Werth's club record with eight consecutive hits. "So, you're able to take that and keep yourself motivated."

Did the Mets, called out last month by the Phils for irritating, over-the-top celebrations after home runs and other clutch moments, get too excited after taking a big lead? Was it something they said? Something they did?

Care to elaborate, Jimmy?

"No, just watch 'em," he said after the Phillies (73–59) reclaimed first place by a half-game. "If you were a player, and you're looking over in that other dugout, you'll feel a certain type of way. Just watch the game."

Okay, that's cryptic.

Clearly, though, the Phillies don't like the Mets. And this comeback began with, of all things, a fifth-inning double by reliever Clay Condrey, a broken-bat scorcher that seemed destined only to provide comic relief amid a six-run deficit before Rollins cracked a two-run homer. And when Ryan Howard swatted a first-pitch fastball into the left-field seats, well, it got serious.

Down to their final out—and their last pinch-hitter—the Phils tied the game against the Mets' rag-tag bullpen on Eric Bruntlett's RBI double. Then, in the thirteenth, they finally won when Shane Victorino roped a leadoff triple and trotted home on a bases-loaded single by Chris Coste, who went 4-for-4 despite starting the game on the bench and entering in the eighth inning.

"A lot of things happened in that game," Charlie Manuel said. "Everything except a fight."

．　．　．　．

It was a character-builder. You really can't tell that you can come back in a game like that until the hits start coming. You have a better feeling when you're down there with the team, but when you're winning 7–0, any team, you feel that one's in the bank,

Shane Victorino scored the winning run in the thirteenth inning against the Mets on August 26. The victory gave the Phillies a half-game lead in the NL East.

and I'm sure the New York Mets felt the same way. To get burned like that takes a little away from you. But you can tell what Jerry Manuel is all about because they always bounce right back. For the Phillies, I think that's a game where you come back and end up feeling and projecting that you should be able to play better for the rest of the season because you were down on the Mets. To come back in the fashion that they did, it shows that character. Guys haven't really gelled the way that they can. Usually, after the All-Star break, everybody starts feeling good and swinging the bats. Well, they haven't gotten hot yet. It's a dogfight. I still say they have their fate in their own hands.

You know, they don't like the Mets. It's the antics, the high-fives, the jumping. [Florida shortstop Hanley] Ramirez said the other day, "We get all the incentive we need just by looking at

[Jose] Reyes." Reyes is a great player, don't get me wrong. But what he doesn't realize is that he's fueling other teams to beat the Mets at any cost because of how he acts. He would probably say, "That's just my style. That's the way that I play." And that's fine. But he gives other teams incentives because of his actions. If he's on your team, you like that. We've said with the Phillies that they need a player to maybe spark some things sometimes. But they're more professional in terms of not showing guys up.

The motivation always comes by doing what you can do to win the ballgame. When you're with the Giants, you didn't like the Dodgers. When you're with the Cubs, you didn't like St. Louis. When you're with Philly, in the days when we played, you didn't like Pittsburgh. It was just common knowledge. Almost like the McCoys and Hatfields. You don't know why. But it's just a dislike. Then, there's certain things that happen on the field, they rub it in your face when they win, and that would be another reason to not like them. That just keeps it going.

I think the series in New York next week is something they're looking forward to. We'll see what happens. The other good thing is they have the benefit of having the pitchers they want, with [Brett] Myers, Jamie [Moyer], and [Cole] Hamels. The last time, it wasn't necessarily like that. Let's face it, the Mets have a damn good team. It's going to boil down to the team that gets hot at the end. Nobody is going to, I think, just run away with it. The thing about the Mets is that they're doing right now what the Phillies aren't. They are hitting the ball, getting big hits. Carlos Delgado. You look at Reyes. You look at [David] Wright, who has been steady all year long. Then, guys like [Carlos] Beltran chip in. And no one is saying anything about their second baseman [Damion] Easley, but he's gotten some big hits against us. And [Fernando] Tatis. You take away some of those guys there, look where we are. But it's going to go down to the last day or so, just like last year.

AUGUST 29, 2008

CHICAGO—Ryan Madson sat at his locker and stared out at nothing.

He was dazed.

And confused.

As much exhilaration as the Phillies felt after Tuesday night's comeback over the New York Mets, that was how despondent they were over last night's loss to the Chicago Cubs at Wrigley Field. Madson inherited a 4–1 lead in the eighth inning and allowed a leadoff home run by Mike Fontenot. Alfonso Soriano crushed a double, Ryan Theriot dunked a single into right field, and after Chad Durbin replaced Madson, Derrek Lee walked and Aramis Ramirez slugged a grand slam that was hit so hard and so far that center fielder Shane Victorino didn't flinch.

6–4 Cubs. Game over.

And while the Phillies (73–62) continue to fret over who will pitch the eighth inning after losing to the Cubs again today 3–2 and falling to two games behind the Mets, Sarge made his singing debut by crooning "Take Me Out to the Ballgame" during the seventh-inning stretch. Wearing a Cubs jersey (a requirement for all guest singers at Wrigley) and holding his grandson, Sarge received a rousing ovation from fans who remember him as the left fielder on their 1984 division-champion team and the hitting coach on the 2003 club that came closer to beating the Florida Marlins and advancing to the World Series than infamous fan Steve Bartman's hand came to left fielder Moises Alou's glove.

. . . .

I played for both teams, and obviously, I'm with the Phillies now, so I had to cover my mouth when it got to the "Root, root, root" part. I've turned them down before, so I had to do it this time. And, really, I think it's an honor that they ask you. There's some people that have been on there quite a few times. [Ron] Santo, he'll go on any time they want. If they can't find somebody, they'll go, "Ronnie, you're it." I have no animosity with them. I wish them well. I mean that sincerely. I have a lot of friends that are on the team. Do I like the way that they treated us [when he was fired as a coach in 2006]? Absolutely not. But the fact is, life goes on. Can't be holding grudges for year in and year out. It just wasn't to be. I had the opportunity, not only as a coach, but as a player, and didn't get it done. So no complaints about that.

I'll always remember 2003 in the sense that, if you look at prior to the playoffs in terms of being able to get a ticket, you could walk right up there. And then, from that season on, it was a difficult time in getting seats. In hindsight, it would've been nice to have one of those rooftops, sit back, and watch the games from there. Things weren't going too well because the Cubs didn't win much until that year. People only remember when you win. The way we ended up losing, yeah, they talk about it some. It wasn't even [Bartman's] fault. Then, I hear Alou say something about he couldn't have caught it. But every time you look at the replay, his glove was up in the air. But it's an instinctive play. How many people in the stands wouldn't have done the same thing? It would've been name-somebody-else if they were in that spot. For me, the better team won that day and that series, plain and simple. Sure, the Marlins had some breaks here and there, but we ended up getting outplayed, and they outhit us. After that play was over with, Alex Gonzalez had a ball go right through his legs that would've gotten us out of the inning. There were a lot of particulars, but nobody ever talks about that because Bartman overshadowed the error that damn near cost us the game, too. We had great pitching. [Matt] Clement had his best year. [Carlos] Zambrano was young Zambrano, pitching well. Kerry Wood and Mark Prior. When you have that good pitching staff, almost like Arizona, man, it makes your .230 hitters think like they're .280s. All of a sudden, they have protection where they're going to damn near shut you down. It's nothing like a legit number one, where you can say, "Okay, guys, we've got this one today." We had that on that team. It was a good time.

AUGUST 31, 2008

CHICAGO—Amid the usual getaway-day bustle—the packing of equipment, the tipping of diligent clubhouse attendants, the overall nuisance of moving an entire team from one city to the next—music blared from a cramped room beneath the stands at Wrigley Field.

It was the sound of the Phillies swaggering out of town.

That's what happens when, after back-to-back demoralizing losses, you rally for consecutive wins over the team with the majors' best record at a ballpark that hasn't been kind to visitors. Indeed, today's 5–3 vanquishing of the Cubs did more for the Phillies than simply salvage an impressive split of a four-game series on the North Side of Chicago. It affirmed, once and for all, how good they can be and demonstrated they can stand with the National League's best.

Sure, the Phillies got a break when Cubs ace Carlos Zambrano was scratched from a start today because of a tired arm. But, during the four games, the Phillies led for 25⅓ innings. The Cubs led for eight. The Cubs didn't have an extra-base hit in the final two games and dropped back-to-back games at Wrigley for the first time since July 25 and 26.

"You have to feel good about it," said right fielder Jayson Werth, who has three home runs and seven RBIs in the past two games and is proving he is capable of playing every day after Geoff Jenkins strained his right hip flexor last week. "They have a good club, and they're real tough at home. But I think we showed we can play with anybody."

. . . .

When this offense is clicking on all cylinders, it's tough to handle. In talking to [Cubs manager Lou] Piniella the other day, he was saying how good this ballclub is. In talking to Billy Williams, he admires the way that [Chase] Utley hits, and also Ryan Howard, with them being left-handed hitters. I said, "To tell you the truth, they aren't hitting the way that they should," and he couldn't believe that they were better hitters than what they were showing against the Cubs. To me, those guys are. It's just being in a slump and going through it. J-Roll is coming out of it now, and look how he's handled himself during the whole thing. Sure, he's disappointed because he hasn't been getting the hits or hitting the ball hard. One thing about J-Roll, when they put the camera on his face, he doesn't look scared. He's probably wondering, "How can this be? How can I go into a slump for this long?" But the fact is, he's out there, he's playing, and this is when players have to recognize that other things in the game they can do to be able to win. He's showed that just defensively. J-Roll does recognize that, and this is the smart thing about this kid, when he's on and doing what he should, the team wins. It's hard to put the emphasis on one particular player, but you know what, it goes with the territory.

The first game of the series, that was just as big a loss as the [13-inning] win they got against the Mets. It's like a punch right in the stomach because that's one of those games that you have in the bank. To lose on home runs, a grand slam, to be outplaying a team the whole game and then lose, it takes a little away from you. That's why I felt that their Saturday game, winning that one, it was a big one. It showed them, hey, we can stand with these guys. We're as good as the Cubs. I think it gave them confidence. Definitely a big series.

. . . .

There was one fewer empty seat on the team charter to Washington.

The Phillies completed a trade yesterday for Matt Stairs, a left-handed-hitting outfielder with 16 seasons of major league experience. Stairs, expected to be used primarily off the bench, was acquired from the Toronto Blue Jays for a player to be named, presumed to be left-handed pitcher Fabio Castro. Stairs, 40, is a .266 career hitter with 252 home runs.

. . . .

I think he's a guy who could help because he could still hit a fastball. That's evident when he gets hold of one. He goes up there with an idea of what he wants to do. Picking him up, for late in the ballgame, it just gives you another option, from a long ball to a base hit. You need that late because you might need that home run. A veteran guy like him, he's been there. He can do that.

Chapter 8

SEPTEMBER

SEPTEMBER 5, 2008

NEW YORK—Mike Schmidt describes himself as a "lucky charm," and after the Phillies lost two of three games to the sad-sack Nationals this week in Washington, he figured they needed to change their luck.

So he sent them an email.

It arrived in Charlie Manuel's in-box this morning, and with the Phillies bracing for an all-important three-game weekend series against the New York Mets at Shea Stadium, Schmidt's 71-word missive found its way to the back of the clubhouse door, where it was posted before batting practice:

> One pitch, one at-bat, one play, one situation, think small, and big
> things result. Tough at-bats, stay up the middle with men on base,

> whatever it takes to keep the line moving. Hot offense. Twenty-seven outs on defense. The Mets know you're better than they are. They remember last year. You guys are never out of the game. Welcome the challenge that confronts you this weekend. You guys are the best.

In other words, win one for the Schmidter.

Like most of the Phillies, Jimmy Rollins was on his way out to the field when he spotted the email. But he skimmed it, and when he came to the part about the Mets, Rollins thought to himself, "Well, that part's true."

"I think it's only natural—if we win three games," Rollins said of the possibility that the Mets are still haunted by last September's collapse. "If not, they'll take a deep breath and get a chance to probably re-gather themselves. But if we win all three games, naturally, you're going to think back to that. It's human nature."

The Phillies took the first step tonight with a 3–0 win behind Brett Myers, masterful again, allowing three hits in eight innings. Greg Dobbs swatted a two-run home run in the seventh to move the Phillies (77–64) within two games of first place in the NL East.

So maybe Schmidt really is a good-luck charm.

"Where was he in '83?" Sarge said, jokingly referring to Schmidt's 1-for-20 snooze in the 1983 World Series loss to the Baltimore Orioles.

· · · ·

Mike is a tremendous athlete, and he's another athlete that would make other players better. He feels by his presence—in the same way I would by being around the guys—that they're going to take something from you, whether or not it's your energy or your sincerity in saying, "Hey, stay back at the plate or do this or do that." Everybody who has played who had some kind of impact would feel that way. But, let's face it, the message that he sent, the guys have really taken it to heart, and they feel very gratified—they feel good—that Mike would send a message like that. That's something that I think really kind of hit home. They looked at it, and they tried to do it. I definitely think it had an impact just because of what some of the players were saying. But keep in mind, in that same way that he can give a lot of fire to the Phillies, he can give that same fire to the New York Mets. It goes hand in hand. It didn't have that effect right away, but you know the Mets players know about it. They heard about it. Hopefully, that doesn't give them some extra motivation. But I know what Mike was probably thinking about. He meant well, and it just goes to show how closely he still keeps up with what the Phillies are doing.

And he's right. No question the Mets are thinking about last year. They have to be. I mean, they choked last year. Plain and simple. It was the worst collapse of all time, worse than the '69 Cubs. So until they win, until they make the playoffs, it's going to get talked about—they're going to get reminded of it. It's going to keep coming up. That's just how it goes.

SEPTEMBER 7, 2008

NEW YORK—When reliever J.C. Romero recorded a double play and ended the matinee portion of today's day-night doubleheader, the Phillies clinched a winning series and assured themselves of gaining at least one game on the division-leading New York Mets.

But they wanted more. They wanted a sweep.

Ambitious? Perhaps. But the Phillies were about to give the ball to ace lefty Cole Hamels, pitching on regular rest, and they always like their chances when Hamels is on the mound.

It didn't happen.

But the Phillies could be in worse shape.

Even after losing 6–3 to split the twin bill and take two of three in their last-ever series at soon-to-be-demolished Shea Stadium, the Phils (78–65) are two games off the Mets' (80–63) pace with 19 games left. Last season, they overcame a seven-game deficit with 17 to play.

. . . .

It was a big game, for sure, being that it was the last time we'll see those guys, and it would've been nice to get a win. But when a particular team has seen you for as long as the Mets have seen Cole, every now and then, they're going to hit you. You won't always be able to beat them up. Sooner or later, they're going to get to you. They know, when you have your number-one guy on the mound, and they score early, that really puts you on your heels right away. And that's kind of what happened.

SEPTEMBER 11, 2008

PHILADELPHIA—As he walked to the plate in the eighth inning tonight, with the Phillies leading by two runs and speedy Shane Victorino at third base, Carlos Ruiz turned to the dugout and asked, "What's the squeeze sign?"

Suddenly, Charlie Manuel had an idea.

"I said, 'Hell, I might as well let him squeeze,'" Manuel recalled. "I figured I might as well start trying to be a National League manager."

Sure enough, Ruiz dropped a bunt, Victorino sprinted home with an insurance run in a 6–3 victory, and the Phillies (80–67) moved within three games of the Brewers in the wild-card standings and shaved the idle New York Mets' division lead to three games.

But, really, they did more than that.

After losing two of three games to the Florida Marlins earlier in the week, backup catcher Chris Coste admitted that he began to doubt that the Phillies would make the playoffs. But by beating Brewers right-hander Ben Sheets, who had not allowed a run in 20 straight innings, they set the tone in the opener of the pivotal four-game series. And with the Brewers refusing to pitch ace lefty CC Sabathia (they're saving him for Monday night's game against the rival Chicago Cubs), the Phillies already are in position to win a series that they absolutely must win.

Ryan Howard, quickly becoming known as Mr. September, stirred the offense with another home run (his majors-leading 43rd) and three more RBIs, and age-less lefty Jamie Moyer started on three days' rest for the first time since July 6, 2004, and pitched 5⅔ gritty innings.

"Somebody had to pitch," Moyer said. "I just felt, why not me? I felt like I was able to throw my name in the hat and let the staff make their choice from that."

. . . .

Now that they beat Ben Sheets, I think they're going to do it. I really do. Beating Sheets really turns it all around. I don't know what's going to happen next, but they beat one of the Brewers' best pitchers. That, right there, would give you incentive that you're not going to face CC, incentive that you beat Sheets, and you take your chances against the rest of the guys who are throwing against you. It was a big game, obviously, getting that very first game. You win that game, and all of a sudden you put so much pressure on Milwaukee because they know they have to go in now and face the Cubs next week. That's the reason they didn't want to start CC. They know how mentally draining that series is. You're talking about a rivalry there. So you beat them in the first game, and now it's just another blow. They know they have to play well the rest of the games just to save themselves from losing the series, or maybe even getting swept.

SEPTEMBER 14, 2008

PHILADELPHIA—Fans, cheering deliriously, waved white rally towels in the air. Jimmy Rollins sped around first base and slid safely into second with a leadoff double. Ryan Howard belted another home run. Pat Burrell picked up run-scoring hits. Brett Myers fired fastballs at overmatched batters.

And, of course, the Phillies won. Twice.

"It kind of felt like last year," Myers said.

If it's September, the Phillies must be making their annual come-from-behind push for the postseason. And on a sweltering Sunday, they took a Bob Beamon–sized leap in that direction with a doubleheader sweep of the reeling Milwaukee Brewers.

By day, Howard swatted a game-tying homer, Burrell laced a go-ahead single, and speedy Shane Victorino broke a 135-at-bat homerless drought with a three-run shot in a 7–3 win. By night, Myers twirled a 95-pitch, two-hit complete game despite pitching on only three days of rest for the first time since October 3, 2004. Rollins reached base five times, Victorino finished 4-for-4, and Burrell went deep for the first time since August 23 in a 6–1 laugher.

Now, after sweeping a four-game series with Milwaukee and winning seven of their last 10 games, the Phillies (83–67) have tied the Brewers (83–67), losers of 10 of 14, for the wild-card lead. They're also only one game behind the division-leading New York Mets (83–65) in the National League East.

May the best team win, just like last year.

"I believe in momentum—whatever you call it—attitude, charisma, when you come to the ballpark, everything is okay," Charlie Manuel said, trying to express the September mood here. "People ain't walking around sulking because they ain't making enough money or something happened at the house."

. . . .

I think they put themselves back in the running, maybe not the driver's seat, but definitely in the running in terms of the games that are left. They needed those games with their backs against the wall just to put themselves back in it with the Brewers. After that, you go on and take your chances. So they made a statement in sweeping because they needed to. Period. I felt that if they could beat Sheets, with the way the rotation was set and being at home, that they'd be ready to go. And they have been. It's just knowing that, looking at the club, looking at the way they're walking around and talking, that was a huge series. Sweeping them gives them a shot in the arm because of the magnitude of the games. These days, who wins a doubleheader? For them to go out and take them out of the game right away, that's key. Take 'em out of the game right away, give them no hope.

SEPTEMBER 16, 2008

ATLANTA—Trailing by one run with a runner on first base and two out in the eighth inning tonight, Ryan Howard walked to the plate against Braves left-hander Mike Gonzalez.

Was there ever any doubt what would happen next?

Ryan Howard hit his 45th home run of the season to lead the Phillies to an 8–7 win against the Braves on September 16.

Howard, baseball's most feared slugger in the midst of a month-long power binge, ran the count full before driving a 93-mph fastball into the left-field seats for his majors-leading 45th home run, the decisive stroke in an 8–7 win that gave the Phillies their fifth-straight victory and nudged them a half-game ahead of the suddenly skidding New York Mets in the NL East.

"I talk about being a carrier, and Ryan's a carrier," Charlie Manuel said after Howard went 4-for-5 and hiked his best-in-baseball RBI total to 136. "He's the guy who knocks in 130 to 160 [runs]. He comes up big in the big moment."

And he always seems to save his best for last. Howard is batting .396 (21-for-53) with eight homers and 22 RBIs in 14 games this month. For his career, he's a .320 hitter with 41 homers, 101 RBIs, and 81 runs in 118 games in the season's final month.

Mr. September, indeed. And with another late-season surge, Howard has played himself into NL MVP consideration, an award that never seemed possible in May when he was batting .163.

"He wants to go to arbitration," Manuel said with a smile, no joke to the Phillies who likely will have to fork over more than the $10 million they paid Howard this season after losing their arbitration case. "I think you see he bears down. He gets after it."

. . . .

There are times, if you look at Ryan, when he strides. Sometimes, he uses a toe-tap. But when he's seeing the ball right, he almost doesn't even have to work on it. You have to realize that it isn't that easy, and this kid has done better than any player who has ever played the game, power-wise, his first three years. That's how we judge guys nowadays. You're talking about this kid maybe winning the MVP, not even hitting .250. That shows you what kind of player he is. This is an era where [batting average] doesn't mean as much. You work on things sometimes in the batting cage, like getting a guy over. But guess what? This guy can hit the ball out of the ballpark at any time. It shows a lot about the kid to come alive in the last few weeks. You've got to say over the years the Phillies have done a pretty good job of getting guys with character. J-Roll, Utley, they are some good character guys. The team has done a good job with that. Let's face it: Howard wasn't hitting early on, at the All-Star break. But one thing he has been consistent with is runners in scoring position. That, in itself, would say something about what kind of player he is, his character. Obviously, nobody likes all of the strikeouts, and I'm sure he doesn't. But everybody likes all the damage he's doing, and basically, he's carrying the ballclub and making the whole lineup better. Down the line, that's going to be a management decision with what to do with Ryan. Obviously, if they wanted to trade him, you've got feel there would be all the teams lined up that would really want him because of the home runs. He's a force to be reckoned with. Put him on the block and see how many people are going to step up.

SEPTEMBER 17, 2008

ATLANTA—J.A. Happ never had time during spring training to worry about earning a spot on the Phillies' pitching staff.

He wasn't around long enough.

Happ, a 25-year-old left-hander, logged four innings in relief before being shipped to minor-league camp in the Phillies' first round of roster cuts. So his contribution to a late-season playoff push—including his first major-league victory here tonight against the Atlanta Braves—has been equally unexpected and gratifying.

"It was awesome," said Happ, offering yet another adjective after collecting ticket stubs, the scorecard, and several game balls. "I understood the position that we're in. I just wanted to get us back in the dugout, keep the momentum on our side, and keep us on the roll we've been on."

After using Jamie Moyer and Brett Myers on short rest last weekend against the Milwaukee Brewers, Charlie Manuel and pitching coach Rich Dubee selected Happ to replace struggling right-hander Kyle Kendrick in the rotation.

The Phillies eased the pressure on Happ by scoring four first-inning runs. Happ, who won the Paul Owens Award as the Phillies' Minor League Pitcher of the Year after posting a 3.60 ERA at Triple-A Lehigh Valley, allowed three hits in six score-less innings in a 6–1 victory that kept the Phillies (85–67) in first place, a half-game ahead of the New York Mets.

．　．　．　．

It's a shot in the arm. When you get games like that, man, it just makes you feel that much better. It was like last year when Kyle came up. Happ looked a lot more comfortable than he did in all the other starts he's made. Absolutely, it was the right decision to go with him over Kendrick, if for no other reason that Happ, being left-handed, proved that he can throw strikes. Keep in mind, he has a curveball and a change-up, whereas it's still a work-in-progress with Kyle.

Kyle, to me, has become predictable. Anyone would be if you only have one pitch. Because then, especially if you can't get it over, hitters will sit on the one pitch. Right now, they're laying off the sinker, and he's not able to get the change-up over, the slider over. It's not going to be a good result. He hasn't been suc-cessful, so I think he's trying to find it. It's almost like he's a lit-tle bit scared with what they're doing to him. He knows he's being counted on to get the job done, so you start thinking, "Oh, man. Is this the start that I'm not going to be starting any-more?" Let's put it this way: if he's not going to come up with another pitch, he's not going to be able to be successful. You've got to have another pitch. It's a must. This isn't even something where you can say, "Maybe I can get away with this or that." It just ain't happening.

SEPTEMBER 21, 2008

MIAMI GARDENS—Rich Dubee didn't have to think for very long.

Asked before today's game if the Phillies' top starting pitchers—Cole Hamels, Brett Myers, and Jamie Moyer—are the best trio that he has ever coached, Dubee shook his head affirmatively. And this is a pitching coach who, with the Florida Marlins in 2001, had Ryan Dempster, Brad Penny, A.J. Burnett, and a young Josh Beckett in his rotation.

"Yeah, but those guys were pretty young, and really, not what they are today," Dubee said. "These guys here are pretty well-established. Even Cole, who is still pretty young, is a much more developed pitcher than some of those guys in Florida were."

Moyer is a sage veteran and, at 45, the majors' oldest player. He's the oldest 15-game winner since knuckleballer Phil Niekro, who at age 46 won 16 in 1985. And by limiting the free-swinging Marlins to one run in six innings today at Dolphin Stadium, he sent the Phillies (88–68) home for the season's final week with a 1½-game lead over the New York Mets in the National League East. Starting with the September 11 victory over the Brewers, they've won nine of 10 games and gained control of their playoff destiny.

• • • •

You have to like the consistency that Jamie Moyer has been bringing, and obviously, Cole could have won a few more games if he got more run support. But I think the jury is still out on how they're going to pitch down the line in the last few games. I don't know that we've really been tested. So in some ways the jury is still out. Sure, the series there with Milwaukee was big, and what they've done here in Florida has been impressive. This is a good-hitting ballclub right here. That's very important. Now, to get back home with a lead [in the division]—just being at home should really propel them.

SEPTEMBER 27, 2008

PHILADELPHIA—Once it was over, after a diving Jimmy Rollins and a spinning Chase Utley impossibly turned the double play that saved the day, Charlie Manuel sat alone in the corner of the Phillies' dugout and let the whole thing wash over him.

"I just looked up and watched the players run on the field and watched the fans' reactions," Manuel said later in the relative quiet of the hallway that leads from the dugout to his office. "I can't explain to you how I felt."

Ecstatic? Absolutely.

Elated? Sure.

Relieved? You bet.

The Phillies, four games out of a playoff spot only 17 days ago, won their second straight National League East crown with a nail-biting 4–3 victory over the Washington Nationals at Citizens Bank Park. As usual, they didn't make it easy. After dropping two games earlier this week against the injury-riddled Atlanta Braves and allowing the bullpen-weary New York Mets to pull within 1½ games, they gave perfect closer Brad Lidge (41-for-41 in save chances) a two-run lead in the ninth inning today. Lidge gave up one run and put the tying run on third base before the big double play—Rollins to Utley to Howard—provided the clincher.

And while champagne flowed in the clubhouse before the frat party–like atmosphere spilled over to the field, the celebration was more subdued this year. Winning the division is great, but the Phillies have more to accomplish.

"In spring training, we were talking about winning the World Series, not just going to the postseason," right fielder Jayson Werth said. "We've still got a job to do. Where we're at is where we always thought we would be."

Added pitcher Brett Myers, "I'm guaranteeing we won't go three-and-out again."

And as remnants of the sellout crowd, once 45,177 strong, lingered in the ballpark and chanted Manuel's name—"Char-lie! Char-lie!"—Manuel finally returned to the field to address his suddenly adoring public.

"Believe me," he said, "we'll go farther than we did last year."

•   •   •   •

If Lidge is in New York, we're not having this conversation. That's how big that closer is. The Mets couldn't close out their games, plain and simple. You can't blame their hitters. The fact is, over there, the hitters are still getting it done.

To me, the [National League] MVP has to be Howard or Lidge. You couldn't have done it without Lidge. But honestly, the way that Howard carried this club, I mean, this doesn't happen like that. This doesn't happen where a guy can carry your whole club. But for the writers who are voting, a lot of times, it's all on the stats. They say, "Well, how do you vote for a guy under .250?" And how do you give it to Lidge when he doesn't have the most [saves]? It's going to be interesting on the vote, but Lidge has to be right there. With [Albert] Pujols, he had a great year there in St. Louis. We just haven't seen him enough.

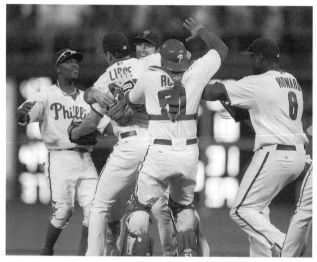

The Phillies celebrated after they clinched their second-straight NL East crown.

In talking with Billy Williams and Ernie Banks, guys like that, they always wonder how they would play under those [playoff] circumstances and what it's like to have champagne poured on you. They've only had the agony of defeat. They've never gone to that other pinnacle and seen the other side. That's why teams that have won it, like the Red Sox, the Yankees, you get a little jealous of that because of the fact that they get to almost take it for granted. What a great feeling to win every year. To get there, after 162, that's not easy. And sometimes, you can almost be overjoyed just to get in and forget that there's more work to be done. With this team, I saw more of a calmness, even in the celebration after it was over. Last year, they were so excited about how they won, how

Jimmy predicted that they were going to win. Then, this year, they won on pure guts. The help they needed was in their own destiny. The biggest games they played all year long were against the Milwaukee Brewers to put them right back in there. Once they beat Milwaukee and Ben Sheets in that first game, and knowing they didn't have to face Sabathia, I thought they were good to go. And, so far, it has been that way.

SEPTEMBER 28, 2008

PHILADELPHIA—By the time most players rolled into Citizens Bank Park today, the champagne bottles were gone. So was the plastic covering over the lockers and, really, any remnants of last night's division-clinching party.

All that was left was for the Phillies was to reflect on winning their second straight National League East crown—and to await their first-round playoff opponent.

So, after the junior varsity—a lineup that didn't include any starters—beat the last-place Washington Nationals 8–3 to close the regular season with a 92–70 record, players returned to the clubhouse to watch, on side-by-side high-definition televisions, the last innings of the Milwaukee Brewers' and New York Mets' games.

Powered by ace lefty CC Sabathia's latest gem on three days' rest, the Brewers edged the Chicago Cubs 3–1 at Miller Park in Milwaukee. A few minutes later, the Mets bowed to the Florida Marlins 4–2 in the last game at Shea Stadium, and for a second year in a row, were eliminated from playoff contention on the season's final day.

Thus, the Brewers (90–72) will be heading to Philadelphia for Game 1 of the best-of-five Division Series, which will open at 3:00 PM Wednesday. They're a fitting opponent, considering the Phils turned around their season two weeks ago with a four-game sweep of the Brew Crew.

Care to make a prediction, Sarge?

. . . .

Well, I'm already getting calls from Milwaukee. They're ready to kick our ass—Phil Rosewicz, their clubhouse guy, and [Hall of Fame broadcaster Bob] Uecker. Isn't it a great thing for baseball to have Milwaukee in it? How about the Rays? It just shows that it's more about the players' character that wins as opposed to having the best team on paper, like Detroit did in spring training. I thought it was sour milk for ownership there with the Yankees to say there's bad division alignments. It's been that way for years. The American League East probably is the toughest league in baseball. But if you can't stand it, you've got to go someplace else.

I don't think you feel any different in the playoffs. I remember when I was with the Cubs in '84, and we were losing near the end of the season, and I called Maddox and went over certain things. He said, "All you've got to do is just go and hit like you always do." Sure enough, I got two game-winning hits in a doubleheader that night and the game-winning hit to clinch [a playoff spot]. So sometimes you just need reassurance. When you're winning, everything gets magnified. Everybody's looking, and a lot of times great players are judged on what they do in the postseason. So it's showcase time. It gives you a chance to see what your players are all about. In talking to the guys, I've been trying to explain that. That's the kind of attitude you've got to have when you go through these play-offs. You've got to have the attitude that, "I'm going to haul off and punch you right in the nose." If you don't have that attitude, it's very difficult to win. The hits are secondary. It's about having good at-bats, squaring the ball up, not bailing, and if you get hits, great. If you don't, you should at least be hitting the ball hard. If you don't, you still should try to do something to help the team at every at-bat. Very simple.

For me, it's all going to be about our two number-one guys: [Cole] Hamels and Brett [Myers]. They've got to win these games here in Philadelphia. In a five-game series, it's just so important to get off to a good start. And it starts with pitching. For hitters, this time of year, it's a frenzy. You throw the wrong type of meat out there, it's going to get eaten up. Those piranhas are going to be waiting right there. It ain't going to happen that you get some mediocre pitcher going through these playoffs. That's why you've got to have at least two pretty good guys going out there. It seems like things are lined up for them. Milwaukee had to have their best guy, [Sabathia], pitch on three days' rest just to get in, although he seems to feel that it doesn't matter. It's old-school with this guy. So if he actually ends up pitching on three days' rest in Game 2, then he gets another start [in Game 5]. I'm looking for the Phils to take two games here. Period. If you've got them down 0–2, that would mean adios. But you've got to win those two games. You've just go to. No excuses.

Chapter 9

THE POSTSEASON

OCTOBER 1, 2008 · NL DIVISION SERIES, GAME 1

PHILADELPHIA—After surviving another white-knuckle ninth inning and securing the Phillies' first postseason victory in 15 years, Brad Lidge pumped his fist and high-fived his teammates.

"What happened to those guys who come out and go 1-2-3?" Jimmy Rollins said.

"I've never been that guy," Lidge said.

"It's never too late to start," Rollins said, flashing his thousand-watt smile.

And so it went, Rollins and Lidge, ribbing each other in the rain, and a rally towel–waving crowd exhaling after a 3–1 victory over the Milwaukee Brewers. No longer do the Phillies have to hear about last season, when they were swept out of the best-of-five Division Series by the Colorado Rockies. They won their first playoff game since October 21, 1993, an all-important victory with imposing Brewers ace CC Sabathia pitching Game 2.

In the series-opener, 24-year-old ace Cole Hamels was marvelous, allowing two hits and striking out nine in eight shutout innings. He was so good, the Brewers were happy to see Lidge in the ninth.

"For Cole to come out and do what he did, it sets the tone for the series," Lidge said. "We really needed to establish that we've got an ace. If people watch Cole Hamels perform start after start, you'll really see something impressive. Hopefully now, he'll get his due as one of the best pitchers in baseball."

. . . .

People who might be saying that Hamels isn't a true number one don't realize, first of all, how young he is. He's still developing. But the fact of the matter is, he could've easily won another five, six games, and then nobody is even questioning or saying anything. If you're talking about the difference between [New York Mets ace Johan] Santana and a Cole Hamels, you're talking only about the experience. You can see it when Santana's out there, and again, Cole Hamels is going to have the same thing. The good thing about it—the experience that he's getting with these playoff games that he's pitching in—is that just makes him that much better. Should people say that Cole Hamels is a legit number one? In today's game, yes. Absolutely.

For me, I just saw more of an overall calmness to the team in the first game. Just getting to this round or the next round isn't enough. These guys want to know what it feels like to be in the World Series. Again, the philosophy has been taking it one day at a time. But they have won and lost as a team for the last two years. Again, the cards they've been dealt, they play them as hard as they possibly can, and it's been pretty damned good up to this point. The Brewers left the door open with a couple of defensive mistakes, and with some clutch pitching from Cole, they ended up winning the ballgame. Again, they didn't score a lot of runs. Hopefully, as the play-offs progress, they'll be able to add on because they're going to have to in order to beat some of the better teams. But, no doubt, it was a good way to start, getting that win and getting that monkey off their backs, so to speak.

OCTOBER 2, 2008 · NL DIVISION SERIES, GAME 2

PHILADELPHIA—In the days before the Division Series began, Milwaukee Brewers ace CC Sabathia had been hailed from Kenosha to Conshohocken as the planet's best pitcher, a 6′7″ left-hander who is both formidable and unbeatable.

Finally, Shane Victorino had enough.

"He's a pitcher," the Phillies' center fielder said. "What am I supposed to say? I'm scared?"

Not quite.

Given no chance to beat Sabathia in Game 2, the Phillies didn't flinch. They worked deep counts, nobody more than pitcher Brett Myers, and forced Sabathia to unleash 98 pitches in 3⅔ innings. And they scored five second-inning runs, powered by Victorino's grand slam, the first in Phillies playoff history.

With their 5–2 win before 46,208 fans—the largest crowd ever in Citizens Bank Park—the Phillies placed the series in a vice grip. Since the creation of the Division Series in 1995, only four teams (none in the NL) have advanced after losing the first two games.

Sabathia—11–2 with a 1.65 ERA after being acquired in a July trade and making a fourth-straight start on three days' rest—was done in by, of all people, Myers. A .116 career hitter and batting with a runner on second, two out, and the game tied 1–1 in the second inning, he fouled off three Sabathia fastballs and worked a nine-pitch walk before Victorino went deep.

"I can't explain it," said Myers, who allowed two runs on two hits in seven innings but will be remembered mostly for his at-bat. "I'm a terrible hitter. It was one of those freakish things."

· · · ·

I didn't know whether or not they were going to beat Sabathia, but again, it was one of those things where they put together good at-bats. They had the right guy up at the right time in Victorino. He has been swinging the bat really well. And he got a pitch and put a good swing on it. That's what it's all about. He wasn't saying, "Okay, I'm looking to hit it out." He was just looking to hit the ball hard. That's all. To me, if that's how their game plan would've been throughout the whole year, you can see the damage that these hitters can do. That's why I've said their best games are ahead of them.

Myers, he had a lot to do with that second inning because there were two outs at the time. For him to foul off that many pitches, and having talked with him after the game, nothing but pure guts enabled him to foul off the pitches that he did. And then, to have the wherewithall to lay off the bad pitches and extend the inning for the top of the order. It was key. He couldn't have been any better. When you have pitchers battle like that, it gives the rest of the team as hitters even more incentive. I used to frown any time the pitcher would get the first hit because that would tell me the guys weren't really doing their job. Now, you put pressure on the rest of the team that says, "Hey, let's go now." That at-bat that Brett had was like, "Let's go."

Did CC run out of gas? Who knows? The one thing you respect about CC, he never made any excuses. He actually said it was his fault and that he didn't make good quality pitches, and that was that. That's why, for me, you don't want to see CC again. The guy has too much pride.

OCTOBER 4, 2008 · NL DIVISION SERIES, GAME 3

MILWAUKEE—Spirits were predictably high on the charter airplane that whisked the Phillies to Wisconsin. A 2–0 lead in the best-of-five Division Series will have that effect.

But if anyone thought winning the series would be a layup, Sarge knew better.

In 1984 Sarge was the left fielder for the Chicago Cubs, who led 2–0 in the best-of-five NLCS before losing three straight to San Diego. And on the flight to Milwaukee, Phillies advisor Dallas Green, the Cubs' GM in 1984, sat next to Sarge and reminisced.

"Don't be afraid to remind these guys what happened to us," Green said.

In Game 3 the Phillies got their own lesson.

The Brewers, presumed to be a dead-team-walking, KO'd Jamie Moyer after four innings, and the Phillies went 1-for-12 with runners in scoring position in a 4–1 loss at Miller Park. Through three games, Chase Utley (2-for-12), Ryan Howard (2-for-8), and Pat Burrell (0-for-8) have been quiet.

And, suddenly, the Brewers have a pulse.

· · · ·

You don't want to make more out of one loss than what it is. If there's an advantage, it's that you're not facing [injured] Ben Sheets or [CC] Sabathia in the next game, and I know a lot of guys have good history against [Game 4 starter Jeff] Suppan. But keep in mind, every major league pitcher can have a hell of a game. You want to close it out. What you don't want to do is go home and have to face Sabathia [in Game 5]. That makes the rest of their team feel better. Absolutely, you give them life if you lose [Game 4], and the pressure begins to mount more to win that last game. These five-game sets, I mean, they're just awful because you can be the best team and be down. Ask the Angels. Ask the Cubs. So I mentioned it to a few guys about what happened to us in '84. I told them, "That can't happen, and it's a bad feeling. You think about it every day. It's not something you ever forget."

OCTOBER 5, 2008 · NL DIVISION SERIES, GAME 4

MILWAUKEE—Jimmy Rollins and Pat Burrell have been teammates since the final month of the 2000 season. But they have known each other since 1994 when Burrell was a strapping high-school slugger from San Jose, and Rollins, a pint-sized shortstop from Oakland, fleeced him in a game of dice.

"That's how I met Pat," Rollins said with a smile.

So, as the Phillies polished off the Brewers today, 6–2, it was only fitting that their longest-tenured players led the way. Rollins, ever the catalyst, launched a leadoff homer in the first inning, hushing a ThunderStix-clapping crowd at Miller Park. Burrell, playing through a lower back strain that nearly sidelined him before Game 1, swatted a three-run homer in the third inning and a solo shot in the eighth to back Joe Blanton's six solid innings.

"I always said, when I got here, I want to change the mentality, change the way people think about the organization," said Rollins, soaked from champagne. "And the only way you can do that is by winning."

. . . .

Pat Burrell took the whole game over. When you hit a three-run homer early like that, it deflates the other club—just a great way to knock them off. How about Charlie [Manuel] saying he isn't thinking about taking Pat out? He has been uncanny about leaving guys in there and coming out smelling like a rose because of the fact that they produce. When Pat took a breaking ball and didn't bail [in the third inning], I said, "Oh, gosh, we've got action." Not knowing he was going to hit the ball, I just knew he was going to have a solid at-bat. Those are the type of at-bats that he has to have to be successful. He's a good enough athlete to do the things that he's doing. But when you have enough of those good at-bats, now, he can put another 30 [batting-average] points up because the consistency is to where it doesn't allow you to go into long, long slumps.

Blanton sure did show me something. He went out, took the bull by the horns, and didn't pitch like he was scared at all. He threw strikes. He threw breaking balls for strikes. He kept them off-balance. Winning that first series is tough, man. You only have five games, and the pressure just keeps going. You don't have time to get back to your number one or number two. They were never able to get back to Sabathia, thank God. He could hardly wait to get another chance. I, for one, am happy they don't have to see him. After being beaten the first three games last year, to come back and do this, it's a feather in their cap. They've improved since last year. They've learned something. That's good. Now they have to keep it going for as long as they can.

.   .   .   .

Next up: the Los Angeles Dodgers.

Last night, the Dodgers finished a surprising three-game sweep of the 97-win Chicago Cubs, favored to win the National League pennant. Energized by a July 31 trade for Manny Ramirez and backed by solid starting pitching from Derek Lowe, Chad Billingsley, and Hiroki Kuroda, the Dodgers have won 22 of their last 30 games. They swept a four-game series against the Phillies in Los Angeles in August, and two weeks later, the Phils won four straight at Citizens Bank Park.

So the series seems to be evenly matched. It also marks a rematch of old rivals. The Dodgers edged the Phillies in the NLCS in 1977 and 1978 before the Phils gained revenge in the 1983 NLCS.

The MVP of that Series: Gary Matthews.

OCTOBER 9, 2008 · NL CHAMPIONSHIP SERIES, GAME 1
PHILADELPHIA—Over the past three days, with the Phillies bracing to play in their first National League Championship Series in 15 years and a region starving for a title, a few fans have honked their horns as they've driven by reliever Ryan Madson's South Jersey home.

"Now I really don't want to screw up," Madson said. "They'll burn my house down."

Madson can rest easy.

After Sarge and Garry Maddox flashed back to the 1983 NLCS victory over the Dodgers by throwing ceremonial first pitches, Chase Utley and Pat Burrell—the sluggers who carried the Phillies' offense in April when Jimmy Rollins was injured and Ryan Howard was slumping—blasted sixth-inning home runs against Dodgers starter Derek Lowe to wipe away a two-run deficit and give the Phillies a 3–2 victory in Game 1 of the best-of-seven series.

But it was Madson, the rail-thin right-hander who emerged last month as the primary eighth-inning reliever, who set down dreadlocked slugger Manny Ramirez on one pitch in the eighth inning to safeguard the one-run lead before Brad Lidge recorded the save for ace Cole Hamels, who improved to 2–0 with a 1.20 ERA in the postseason.

. . . .

Manny Ramirez set a tone right away with that double off the top of the [center-field] wall to let people know he was going to be reckoned with. You've got to give credit, however, to Cole Hamels to be able to settle down and keep his club in a situation where they could be able to come back and score some runs. Chase came up with just a clutch, tying home run, and then you end up having Pat come up with the game-winning home run. That's really what it's all about. Lidge was Lidge. Madson continues to impress. I remember early in the season, it was like, where's the velocity or is this a guy you can try to trade? Thank God they didn't because his velocity has gotten up to 95, 96, with that filthy change-up. That makes the difference. But they're to be commended on that game. It was a complete team effort.

I'm very happy, especially with me and Maddox throwing out the first pitch. You know, we're competitors. Obviously, you're not playing in the game, but we don't want that on our watch. We don't want to be held responsible for any losses. I think what I'll do is have Pat Burrell sign that ball since he had the game-winning hit, plus he plays left field and he's one of my guys. J-Roll and Ryan, you couldn't have this club without those guys. But to see Pat, after the second half that he's had, play the way that he did, that's really what it's all about. Just like when Aaron Rowand left as a free agent, you don't think about it until afterward. But Pat has been one of the best players that the Phillies have ever had, and he isn't gone yet, but he's still a class act.

OCTOBER 10, 2008 · NL CHAMPIONSHIP SERIES, GAME 2

PHILADELPHIA—They stood, waving white rally towels, and with all their breath, they cheered, repeating the same two-syllable chant in rhythmic harmony.

"Beat L.A.! Beat L.A.!"

Then, for the second straight game, the Phillies complied.

But this 8–5 victory, which gave the Phils a commanding 2–0 lead over the Dodgers in the best-of-seven NLCS, wasn't always pretty. The offense belched out a pair of four-run rallies fueled by, of all people, pitcher Brett Myers, who collected three hits and three RBIs.

And it was hardly festive. About 4½ hours before the game, Charlie Manuel learned that his 87-year-old mother, June, passed away in a Roanoke, Virginia, hospital, one day after undergoing an angioplasty. And when the game was over, center fielder Shane Victorino got word that his 82-year-old grandmother had died in Hawaii.

So although the Phillies' traveling party (including Manuel and Victorino) boarded a flight to Los Angeles with favorable odds to advance to the World Series for the first time since 1993, nobody was in the mood to celebrate.

"I can't even imagine what they must be going through," third baseman Greg Dobbs said.

"I guess this is Black Friday, after all," added Myers, the eighth pitcher with three hits in a playoff game and the first to have three hits and three RBIs since Cincinnati's Dutch Ruether in the infamous 1919 World Series that was lost on purpose by the Chicago White Sox.

. . . .

Obviously, everyone's prayers and condolences go out to Charlie and Shane and their families. You just try to make sure that they know people are behind them and thinking about them. Honestly, this club plays hard for Charlie no matter what. It's a terrible loss, to lose your mother. And Charlie has done a heck of a job this year. He gets a lot of blame around here when things aren't right. The thing is, he's articulate when it comes to speaking with his players and motivating them. As a manager, if you can get the best ability out of your players, that's what it's all about. This year, he's stuck with guys when people were questioning him. Why are you playing Ryan Howard as much? Because when he does damage, nobody else has to hit. So he stuck with him, same as he did for [Jayson] Werth or for Pat Burrell. When he's able to discipline people, he's able to do it in his own way. I respect it because he doesn't use the paper to do that. Dallas was just the opposite. If you're weak at heart, you're going to leak all over yourself with some of the things he said about you. He'd have you in black print if you weren't doing the job. It's a different age now, though. We would use it as a motivation. The players of today, they'll be like, "I'll let you know when I want to play the game." But I thought the mood after the game was really good, considering everything that went on off the field.

With Brett getting the three hits, it shows you that anybody who goes up there and swings has a chance to get a hit. I mean, Stevie Wonder has as good a chance of hitting that ball. That just goes to show, not only is it a humbling game, but you never know what's going to happen. He's the last guy that you'd ever say was going to get three hits, and they happened to be big hits, and they needed all of them, especially in the way that he got them. No question, it demoralizes the other team. But nobody is like, "Oh, we've got it made." Not at all. I think they realize they've got a lot of games still to go.

OCTOBER 12, 2008 · NL CHAMPIONSHIP SERIES, GAME 3

LOS ANGELES—As Shane Victorino walked to the plate in the sixth inning, 56,800 fans—the largest crowd in the 46-year history of Dodger Stadium—booed loudly.

Who said it's more laid back in La La Land?

Three innings earlier, Victorino, the Phillies' excitable center fielder, had helped to incite a benches- and bullpens-clearing dust-up after Dodgers starter Hiroki Kuroda tossed a pitch over his head, an apparent retaliation for Brett Myers's fastball near Manny Ramirez's noggin early in Game 2. By then, though, the Dodgers already had made a more powerful statement about the best-of-seven NLCS.

It's not over. Not by a long shot.

Only two teams have recovered from a 0–2 deficit to win the NLCS, but the Dodgers scored a resounding 7–2 victory and breathed life into their postseason chances. They blitzed 45-year-old lefty Jamie Moyer, KO'ing him after only 1⅓ innings, his shortest start since July 4, 1998, and the Phillies' offense mustered just five hits. Moyer is 0–2 with a 13.50 ERA during the postseason.

"Momentum is definitely a big thing," Victorino said, "but it's one game."

. . . .

I think you've got to go from exactly how it started, and it was the ball that was thrown behind Manny Ramirez, which was high. It wasn't at his head, but the intent was to intimidate. Put it this way, if I'm playing, I'm thinking that was on purpose. So their guy did the same thing to Victorino. That doesn't make it wrong. As a teammate, he gets instant respect. The fact is, Kuroda took the Phillies out of the game to where they didn't have good at-bats. You just hope it doesn't change the series.

Jamie just could never get started. They centered a lot of balls. And the balls they hit, they found holes. Whether or not he pitches again, I think it comes back to what they think will give them the best chance to win. He's not going to strike out guys. So he's got to have pitches that are called. In winning 16 games, it'll tell you that he's done it most of the time. But it's a tough call for a guy who's been there for you. The player is going to feel like, "Hey, all I did for you and you can't stick with me?" I'm glad I don't have to make that decision.

OCTOBER 13, 2008 · NL CHAMPIONSHIP SERIES, GAME 4
LOS ANGELES—Matt Stairs hasn't been the most practiced hitter lately, getting only two at-bats through the Phillies' first seven playoff games. And in 16 seasons in the majors he had never faced hard-throwing Dodgers closer Jonathan Broxton.

But the scouting report on Broxton is simple. His best pitch, the one he throws in any tight situation, is his blazing fastball, which often reaches into the upper 90s. Stairs, meanwhile, is a classic fastball hitter, and his approach at the plate is even more simplistic.

Grip it and rip it.

So after Broxton got behind in the count, Stairs turned on a 95-mph heater on the inner half of the plate, launching it into the pavilion over the right-field wall. It was the biggest homer of Stairs's career, and it broke a tie, giving the Phillies a come-from-behind 7–5 victory.

"In hockey, you shoot as hard as you can, so I've always figured, why not swing as hard as I can," said Stairs, a short, stocky, 40-year-old wannabe hockey player from Canada. "In batting practice, I try to hit every ball out of the ballpark. I'm not going to lie. I try to hit home runs, and that's it."

Three batters before Stairs's blast, Shane Victorino, Public Enemy Number One in Los Angeles after his Game 3 flare-up with Dodgers starter Hiroki Kuroda, belted a game-tying two-run home run into the Phillies' bullpen.

And just like that the Phillies are one win from reaching their first World Series since 1993.

•   •   •   •

Big game. Huge game. The fashion in which they came back to win just let all the air out of the Dodgers' sails. They're just about spent. That was a game they had on their ledger. Victorino coming back and hitting a home run, and then you have Matt Stairs coming up and hitting the game-winning home run—with two outs mind you—just about deflated that ballclub. They're just about done. With the damage that Victorino is doing, you'd be like, "There's your MVP." The hits that he's gotten are big hits.

As a team, they're not hitting on all cylinders like we've seen before, but they're doing what you need to do to win.

Everybody in baseball knows Stairs is a fastball hitter. Look at him in batting practice. He swings to hit home runs. He's a little more under control because he'll hit balls out toward left or right-center. He'll pull balls. But he knows that he has that one shot to get a fastball and see ya later. In that particular case, though, it's like Broxton said, "Okay, here's my best," and Stairs was up to the task. Let's face it, in that situation, you can pop it up, you can swing through it. The guy is throwing 98. There was no doubt about it. You could see their heads drop after that. It'll knock you out. TKO. What it does, it makes you think about that loss a lot longer than if you got beat 14–2. This is like, what could've been? It was right there.

OCTOBER 15, 2008 · NL CHAMPIONSHIP SERIES, GAME 5

LOS ANGELES—At last, Bill Giles's dream has come true.

For years, Giles has presented the trophy named for his late father to the team that wins the National League pennant. And, for years, he has stood in a clubhouse reeking from champagne, surrounded by euphoric players, and wished only that someday he could hand the trophy to his beloved Phillies.

On a warm Wednesday night in Southern California, he finally could.

Sparked by a leadoff home run by Jimmy Rollins, fortified by an opportunistic offense that capitalized on three fifth-inning errors, and backed by seven masterful innings from ace Cole Hamels, the Phils finished the Dodgers 5–1 in Game 5 of the NLCS. For the first time since 1993—and only the sixth in their 126-year history—the Phillies are World Series–bound next week against either the Boston Red Sox or the Tampa Bay Rays.

"To be able to hand the trophy to the guy I hired to run the club [team president David Montgomery]," said Giles, the Phillies' chairman, "to see how he has grown, to see how hard they played, to know how much this means back home, it's unbelievable."

Nearly every player partying in the cramped visitors' clubhouse at Dodger Stadium had his moment in the NLCS triumph. Mostly, though, the Phils did it with shut-down pitching (Hamels was named NLCS MVP), well-timed home runs, and of course heavy hearts.

"The last time I talked to my mom, she said, 'Pray for me,'" Charlie Manuel said. "Then, she said, 'Charles Jr., you're going to win these games and go to the World Series.' That's the last thing she said to me."

. . . .

I read the lineups [for Fox television] before the game, and I did it the very first take. Perfect. Phone rings. I had to do it over again. Took me about four or five takes. It was like, to hell with the nicknames. No "Flyin' Hawaiian." No "Pat the Bat." I went straight to it. It's not as easy as you think when those lights get on you. At least it wasn't an omen for the game. Getting off right away with J-Roll, and the way Cole pitches, they had a feeling they can't come back. That was a big-game pitcher winning the ballgame. That's what it's all about. His whole demeanor, and even though things might go bad in the course of the game, he's not showing it out on the mound. He's beyond his years. Everybody has said that, and he's proving that in these playoffs.

I went down there [to the clubhouse] a little later on, not to get all well, but to congratulate the guys. It's just a great

Jayson Werth and the Phillies celebrated after defeating the Dodgers in the NLCS and punching their ticket to the World Series.

accomplishment for the Fightin' Phils. You can't call that luck. They put a whipping on the Dodgers, and it did my heart some good. Now, we're even [in the NLCS], 2–2. Collectively, as a group, they were doing it. They played really good defense. They got excellent pitching, and once they got the ball to Lidge, that has been their formula all year long. The guys have accomplished some things that it has taken guys a lifetime to get to. Cole has been here three years. I mean, guys don't realize, and they will later on, how special it is to be in a World Series because some guys never get there. I've been around Ron Santo, Billy Williams, Ferguson Jenkins, and they always wonder how they would play and never got that chance. It's a special, special time. So, I'm just really happy for these guys. It's well deserved.

OCTOBER 22, 2008 · WORLD SERIES, GAME 1

ST. PETERSBURG, Florida—There were times during the opening game of the 104th World Series when the cowbells and the music and the artificial noise grew so head-splittingly loud underneath the Tropicana Field dome that you scarcely could hear yourself think.

The Phillies loved every minute of it.

En route to winning a division championship, the Phils posted a 44–37 road record, best in the National League. By now, they know how to kill the locals' buzz. So as the sellout crowd of 40,783 roared for the upstart Tampa Bay Rays, baseball's 2008 feel-good story, Chase Utley landed a collective gut punch with a two-run homer in the first inning. Then ace left-hander Cole Hamels lulled everyone into submission for seven innings.

And when Brad Lidge closed out another ninth inning and secured the Phillies' 3–2 victory, he hit the proverbial mute button.

"Being on somebody else's home turf," Hamels said after the Phillies won despite going 0-for-13 with runners in scoring position, "I think you have to take a step back, no matter how loud it gets, and just focus on the next pitch."

On the road, no team does it better than the Phillies.

·   ·   ·   ·

It just shows you how different guys really step up. It was a big lift when Chase hit that home run. People could put those cowbells right down on the ground. Those things don't affect good athletes. You zone 'em out. But it was loud. I thought it was irritating and offensive to have people clanging those damn bells. That's why it was so good when Chase shut them up.

You know, the World Series is different. It's a big deal. It's a huge thing. It's a seven-day Super Bowl. The accomplishment to get from spring training to this point, I mean, how special is that. There are going to be some heroes here, and there are going to be some guys here who might get ripped. Funny things can happen. Ask one of my friends, Bill Buckner. I remember that I had butterflies before all the World Series games in '83. But once it starts, you settle down. I had made up my mind that I was taking the first pitch, period. Just to settle down, see a pitch, get your game plan down. Chase, obviously, had a good game plan. He knew what he was doing up there, and he squared up a ball and hit it hard. And then Cole, well, he kept doing what he's been doing. He's been just terrific. What more can you say? It was big, getting that first game, especially on the road. It's a good way to start.

OCTOBER 23, 2008 · WORLD SERIES, GAME 2

ST. PETERSBURG, Florida—From the time they're in Little League, it's every player's dream to line up on the field and be introduced before a World Series game.

That didn't happen before Game 1.

At the behest of Fox television, Major League Baseball shortened the pregame introductions, limiting them to only the starting lineups. Several Phillies players were upset, and they have requested that they be announced before Game 3 at Citizens Bank Park on Saturday night.

Meanwhile, they have bigger problems.

The Phillies went 1-for-15 with runners in scoring position tonight and fell to the Rays 4–2 at Tropicana Field. They are 1-for-28 in that situation during the first two games, and suddenly, by the grace of only Cole Hamels's Game 1 gem, the Series is tied as it shifts to Philadelphia.

"We've done this before, unfortunately," Rollins said, referring to the 10-week team-wide mid-season slump in which the Phillies struggled to pick up clutch hits. "But, fortunately, we have done this before, so we know how to get out of it."

. . . .

I thought maybe they weren't seeing the ball as well in the dome. It's difficult to pick the ball up in any of the domes, period. You get used to it when you're playing here, and the guys who come in with the road team, sometimes it takes a little more time to get used to it. But no excuses. The guys just aren't hitting. They're getting guys on base, so it's not a total loss. They just need to start coming up with the big hits at the big times.

On the introductions, I definitely see where they're coming from. The only people who don't understand are the people who haven't been through a 162-game season. It's awful not to be recognized, from your clubhouse guy on up. How about cutting out some of those commercials? At least give them their due. I feel exactly the way the guys did, or worse, because I know what it's like to be down there. The guys who start, like I did, can take it for granted. But to hear your name in an arena like this does wonders, just the feeling of being recognized.

OCTOBER 25, 2008 · WORLD SERIES, GAME 3

PHILADELPHIA—Jamie Moyer waited 22 years to pitch in a World Series.

He hardly minded another 91 minutes.

So Moyer paced around the Phillies' clubhouse, stretched his left arm, and did anything to stay loose for a game that, one day earlier, he called "the biggest start of my life." And once it began, at 10:06 PM, after the rain ceased, he mowed down the Rays' hitters for six innings.

It wasn't enough.

Neither were solo homers by Carlos Ruiz, Chase Utley, and Ryan Howard, who ended a 42-at-bat homerless drought. To complete a stirring 5–4 win, at 1:47 AM, the Phils needed Ruiz's 30-foot swinging bunt down the third-base line and a mad dash to home plate by Eric Bruntlett in the bottom of the ninth on a night when a few of late closer Tug McGraw's ashes were spread on the mound by his son, Tim, before the game.

"If it's a hit, I'll take it," Ruiz said after getting only the Phillies' second hit in 33 chances with runners in scoring position and giving them a 2–1 lead in the Series. "It was a great moment I'll remember for the rest of my life."

Should the Phillies win two more games, Ruiz will have a moment to top it.

.   .   .   .

The big man, Ryan Howard, capitalized on a hanging break-ing ball. Utley showed you the hitter he can be. You got to mention Ruiz with the way he's been swinging. But what stuck out for me was Jamie Moyer's focus. Not telling anybody that he was sick and going out and pitching. You remember with the Chicago Bulls, Michael [Jordan] had a temperature of 100-something, and people were saying it's the worst news they could hear because he'd probably play his best game. Same thing with Jamie. With so much talk about whether or not they should pitch him because of how he pitched earlier in the playoffs, Jamie proved everyone wrong once again. Being sent down to the minors after being in the major leagues [in 1992], and finding his way back, that right there tells you the character of Jamie Moyer. And the [diving] play that he made on [Carl] Crawford, that was pure emotion, pure effort. That's what you preach about.

With what Tim McGraw did, it got really emotional for me. Knowing what Tug McGraw meant to the organization, I thought it was a really good touch. It was like Tug McGraw's here, and I would think we need all the good omens that we possibly can get.

OCTOBER 26, 2008 · WORLD SERIES, GAME 4

PHILADELPHIA—Two days after the All-Star Game and two weeks before the July 31 trade deadline, the Phillies sent three minor leaguers to Oakland for Joe Blanton, a burly right-hander with a barely .500 career record.

Around baseball, the move was met with yawns.

Tonight, in Game 4 of the World Series, Blanton woke everybody up.

He did it with his right arm, chucking fastballs past the Rays hitters. And he did it—in unexpected fashion—with his bat, becoming the 15th pitcher to homer in the World Series and the first since Oakland's Ken Holtzman in 1974. Thus, Blanton led the Phillies to a 10–2 victory and the brink of their first World Series crown since 1980.

Not bad for a so-called consolation prize.

"All of the critics talked about Joe's ERA or his win-loss ratio in the first half of the season," pitcher Brett Myers said. "But I'll take a guy with a lot of heart, and Joe has a lot of heart. He's been an asset to this team."

Ryan Howard slugged two homers and collected five RBIs, and Jayson Werth went deep. Meanwhile, Rays sluggers Carlos Pena and Evan Longoria are a combined 0-for-29 in the Series.

.   .   .   .

Any time a pitcher hits a home run, there's just no justice. Really. You get guys that hit, hit, hit, and he comes up and hits every now and then and hits a ball out. It just goes to show that you're a dangerous guy if you're swinging the bat. Obviously, the pitcher supplied the power. But you've still got to hit it. On the mound, Joe was strong. He had a downward plane on his ball. He kept the ball out of the middle of the plate, for the most part. I don't think we really have seen the real Joe yet. There were a lot of starts there, early on, where he was just giving them five innings. Has he pitched the way that they thought he would? I think they're happy, but you're always happy when you're winning. If he maybe wasn't the best out there, he was still better than what they had. In coming here from day one, Joe said guys really welcomed him like he'd been here forever. I've been traded before, and it helps when you walk into that clubhouse and they're with you right away.

I think that when Ryan starts to swing like that, it has not that much to do with getting in a groove as it does with hitting a pitch that's up in the zone. Ryan probably gets himself out more than the pitcher gets him out by forcing the action. He did an excellent job of going out and hitting the ball to left. He stayed back on the ball and cold-cocked it. That's why Charlie doesn't like taking him out of the lineup. He can hit it out of Yellowstone. That's a back-breaker. Then he comes back, and bam, hits it again. They opened up a can of whip-ass on them. They needed it, too.

OCTOBER 27, 2008 · WORLD SERIES, GAME 5

PHILADELPHIA—On the night the drought finally could've ended, there was a flood.

The heavens opened, and for six innings, a fine mist became a steady rain that grew into a heavy downpour. The umpires, at the urging of Major League Baseball, waited for as long as they could. But the infield turned to mud, and Citizens Bank Park looked more like Noah's Ark.

So for the Phillies and their tormented fans, the wait continued.

After the Tampa Bay Rays tied the game 2–2 in the top of the sixth inning, the umpires finally called for the tarp. The game was suspended, and it'll pick up where it left off tomorrow night, weather-permitting, although more rain is in the forecast. It marked the first time a World Series game had been suspended.

And it wasn't without controversy. The Phils were upset over losing ace lefty Cole Hamels, whose final start of the postseason was truncated after only 6⅓ innings. They also weren't happy that the Rays were allowed to bat in the sixth, and on the muddy field, Jimmy Rollins couldn't make a play on B.J. Upton's grounder up the middle. One batter later, Upton scored the tying run.

"Rollins, more than likely with a dry field, he would get to that ball," Charlie Manuel said.

· · · ·

No doubt about it, J-Roll gets to that ball. But the fact is, you've still got to be able to hit the ball. No matter, to me, the commissioner got it right. You don't want a World Series to be tainted by only five innings. Whether or not it's before or after, whether or not they tied it, kudos for them. It's easy to sit back and fire shots. Put yourself in that position. You're never going to make everybody happy, but you have to do what's right. Now, should he have maybe stopped it in the fourth when he could've played a full nine? Well, we have Cole Hamels there. So, for me, to restart it where it is, "Okay, let's go." The commissioner had nothing to do with the weather. He knew one thing: they had to play nine innings, come hell or high water. To win it in less than nine innings, I wouldn't feel good. To lose it, I would feel awful.

It's like Christmas Eve when you know you can clinch it. You can't sleep at night. I'm sure the guys couldn't wait to get to the ballpark. When you win it, that's something they can never take away from you. Those are memories you'll be able to share with your kids and grandkids. I have confidence. But I had confidence in '84 with the Cubs. I'm not counting any chickens until they hatch and the chickies are walking. Been there, done that. You're on the threshold, but when the final out is done, that's when you talk about it. I brought an extra shirt tonight, and one of my least favorite hats. That would be something I would go down there for. The other celebrations they were asking, "Hey, where were you?" They were looking to douse me. I thought it was anticlimactic for me because I had gone through it before. But this, if they win, that would be something new for me. But I'm not saying anything until it is completely over.

OCTOBER 29, 2008 · WORLD SERIES, GAME 5 (RESUMED)
PHILADELPHIA—It took 28 years—and then 46 hours for suspended-by-rain Game 5 to resume—but the Phillies finally won another World Series, vanquishing the upstart Rays 4–3, and kicking off a celebration across the Delaware Valley.

The Phillies are world champions.

At last.

At 9:58 PM, on a cold Wednesday night in late October, with flashbulbs popping before each pitch, the moment actually occurred. Closer Brad Lidge, the Phillies' Mr. Perfect, struck out Eric Hinske, dropped to his knees, and was swarmed on the mound by his teammates.

Fireworks exploded overhead, and the 50-foot Liberty Bell swung and clanged in right field. A sellout crowd—and a city that hadn't celebrated a major pro sports championship since 1983—went delirious.

Pedro Feliz, the slick-fielding third baseman, delivered the championship-clinching hit in the seventh inning, a single through Tampa Bay's drawn-in infield against side-winding reliever Chad Bradford. Pinch-runner Eric Bruntlett, who entered after free-agent-to-be Pat Burrell's leadoff double, dashed home from third base. Cole Hamels, once again, earned MVP honors.

And now Hamels and Howard, Utley and Rollins, and all the rest stand alongside Schmidt and Carlton, Bowa and McGraw, and the legends of 1980 whom they have heard so much about.

"We wanted to change the face of the organization," Ryan Howard said. "We did that. We're losers no more. The organization is a bunch of winners, and nobody can take that away from us."

. . . .

I've got to think that anyone who has been with the Phillies or played with the Phillies was just extremely happy. I only went to the World Series the one time and did not win, so the feeling you get from the first pitch, not even being down there, you were just excited to be able to go on the ride with the guys. What an accomplishment. You're happy for all of them. Sure,

Finally! The Phillies claim their first World Series championship since 1980.

they had a great team, but no one was saying that were going to win the World Series. You always hope. It was the way the ball bounced. What if we split with Milwaukee in September? They were so resilient, and they ended up winning.

I think what helped them more than anything was that they were able to have Cole Hamels, their number-one guy, for all the big games with the full amount of rest, and with the bullpen, the pitching was just phenomenal. In the last game, Geoff Jenkins coming up with the double and Pat Burrell getting up and hitting a double, those are huge. [Carlos] Ruiz didn't have his best year, but the contribution he made during the playoffs had to make you feel good and showed you what he was really all about. Guys like Jamie Moyer, whose career started in '87, you can't help to feel good for him. The fans probably will remember forever that play when he dove and caught the ball off of [Carl] Crawford.

That one pitch from Lidge to close it out just made people so happy. You recognize that you don't do this every single year. It's so tough. You're happy for Charlie with the way things went. In their meetings with him in previous offseasons, [team president David Montgomery] joked that he'd only taken as high as second place. And he mentioned in his speech that he didn't have second place anymore. You're talking Division Series and Championship Series and then the World Series. That's a lot to go through. I told J-Roll, "You're probably not going to realize what this means until you come back and they give you a standing-O because fans here, they don't forget."

It's a passionate city, evident by the parade. There's no way you can talk about how many people—one million, two million—were there because you'd be guessing. It was just so many people, young and old. No one could picture the magnitude of that. People were saying that this parade blew the '80 parade away. Just blew it away. It'll be something that I'll never, ever forget. Someday, when I tell my grandson about this season, the first thing I'll say, well, it was indescribable.

Acknowledgments

Thank you to my mother, Catherine Matthews, for always teaching me to follow my dreams, and to my two grandsons, Gavin and Denver—may all your dreams come true.

—Gary Matthews

In 10 years of covering sports for newspapers, and especially the past three as a Phillies beat writer, writing a book has always been a goal. But it took a host of people to make this a reality.

Thanks to Tom Bast, editorial director at Triumph Books, for finding me, and Adam Motin, who prodded me toward the book's conclusion. Sports editor Jason Levine and executive editor David Ledford at *The News Journal* supported this undertaking and trusted that it would not be a distraction. Several colleagues offered help, including *Camden Courier-Post* beat writer Michael Radano and Martin Frank, my teammate at *The News Journal*. And many thanks to Dave Smith at Retrosheet.org and the fine folks at Baseball-Reference.com, who offer invaluable resources to baseball writers everywhere.

But, of course, were it not for the performance of the 2008 Phillies and the cooperation of "Sarge," Gary Matthews, this book never would have been possible.

—Scott Lauber

About the Authors

GARY MATTHEWS

Known around baseball as "Sarge" because of his habit of saluting the fans in the left-field bleachers at Wrigley Field, Gary Matthews spent 16 seasons in the majors with the San Francisco Giants, Atlanta Braves, Philadelphia Phillies, Chicago Cubs, and Seattle Mariners. He was the NL Rookie of the Year in 1973 and MVP of the 1983 NL Championship Series. Presently, he's a television analyst for Phillies games. He lives in Chicago with his wife, Sandra, and has four children: sons Gary Jr., Delvon, Dustin, and Dannon, and daughter Paige.

SCOTT LAUBER

A New Jersey native and Boston University graduate, Scott Lauber just completed his third season as the Phillies' beat writer for the *Wilmington* (Del.) *News Journal*. Previously, he covered the New York Mets' minor league system for the *Binghamton* (N.Y.) *Press & Sun-Bulletin*. His work has appeared in *Sports Illustrated*, and he won an Associated Press Sports Editors award in 2005.